SELF-GOVERNANCE IN COMMUNITIES AND FAMILIES

SELF-GOVERNANCE

IN

COMMUNITIES

AND

FAMILIES

GARY M. NELSON

BERRETT–KOEHLER PUBLISHERS, INC.
San Francisco

Berrett-Koehler Publishers, Inc.
450 Sansome Street, Suite 1200
San Francisco, CA 94111-3320
Tel: (415) 288-0260
Fax: (415) 362-2512
www.bkconnection.com

Printed in the United States of America

 Printed on acid-free and recycled paper that is composed of 50% recovered fiber, including 10% post consumer waste.

ORDERING INFORMATION

Quantity sales. Special discounts are available on quantity purchases by corporations, associations, and others. For details, contact the "Special Sales Department" at the Berrett-Koehler address above.

Individual sales. Berrett-Koehler publications are available through most bookstores. They can also be ordered direct from Berrett-Koehler: Tel: (800) 929-2929; Fax: (802) 864-7626; www.bkconnection.com

Orders for college textbook/course adoption use. Please contact Berrett-Koehler: Tel: (800) 929-2929; Fax: (802) 864-7626.

Orders by U.S. trade bookstores and wholesalers. Please contact Publishers Group West, 1700 Fourth Street, Berkeley, CA 94710. Tel: (510) 528-1444; Fax (510) 528-3444.

Library of Congress Cataloging-in-Publication Data
Nelson, Gary M.
     Self-governance in communities and families/by
     Gary M.Nelson.—1st ed.
          p. em.
     Includes bibliographical references and index.
     ISBN 1-57675-086-8
     1. Social action—United States. 2. Social participation—United States. 3. Community organization—United States. 4. Human services—United States—Citizen participation. 5. Public-private sector cooperation—United States. I. Title.
     HN65 .N43 2000
     361.2'5'0973—dc21   99-086444

First Edition
     05   04   03   02   01   00   10   9   8   7   6   5   4   3   2   1

CONTENTS

ACKNOWLEDGMENTS

This book is dedicated to my family for their love, support, and teachings.

My parents taught me the principles and values of self-governance—responsibility for self and service to others. They taught me by example. I thank them.

My wife Geri taught me about relationships and provided me with critical reflections on the manuscript. I am a better person because of my relationship with her, and the book has benefited also. This book, like a good marriage, is about relationships and dialogue for a common purpose—the well-being of the family with the support of the community.

My children—Alec, Alexis, Alicia, and Aaron—continue to teach and remind me of the important things in life. They enrich my life immeasurably. They also challenge me to live up to my values. I have not always been successful, but I have always tried. It is from them that I derive a sense of future, hope, and inspiration. I am proud of them all.

This book is also dedicated to my colleagues and friends for their support and contributions to my larger family—my neighborhood and my work community. I want to thank them for their support and contributions to this book. They include:

- All the great people at the Jordan Institute for Families for their friendship, good humor, and dedication to service

- My neighbors and friends in Stratton Park, a neighborhood oasis in Raleigh, North Carolina, for their friendship and support

- The individuals with whom I have had the pleasure to facilitate self-governance dialogues across the state of North Carolina and throughout this country—Lane Cooke, Amy D'Aprix, Audley Donaldson, Chris Howell, Yvette Murphy, Debbie Vassar, Paul Vivian, and Linda Rahija

- The dedicated public servants and citizens who do the hard work of strengthening communities and families day in and day out; I stand in admiration of their commitment, their heart, and steadfastness

- Valerie Barth, a senior editor at Berrett-Koehler Publishers, Inc., for her original and continuing support of this book

- And Charlie Dorris, the freelance developmental editor, with whom I worked during the early stages of this book. Charlie, through his gentle spirit and insights, encouraged me to trust my own voice and through his technical skills helped polish that voice

Self-Governing Communities and Families

When I was young and free and my imagination had no limits, I dreamed of changing the world. As I grew wiser, I discovered the world would not change, so I shortened my sights somewhat and decided to change only my country. But it too seemed immovable. As I grew into my twilight years, in one last desperate attempt, I settled for changing only my family, those closest to me, but alas, they would have none of it. And now as I lie on my deathbed, I suddenly realize: If only I had changed myself first, then by example, I would have changed my family. From their inspiration and encouragement, I would then have been able to change my country and, who knows, I may even have changed the world.

—Anglican bishop, Westminister Abbey, 1100 A.D.

What are the lessons of the bishop's parable for community and family self-governance? For me the lesson is that the essence of community is found or not found in the individual—each one of us. Community exists where individuals first exercise responsibility for their own well-being and then through service, a reciprocal responsibility to contribute to the well-being of others. A sense of community when found in neighborhoods, cities, regions of the country, or in an organization is the collective expression of individual values and practices.

Self-governance in turn is the decision-making process whereby communities and families exercise authority and control over themselves. It is the process by which we steer our many selves—as parent, professional, or citizen—toward self-rule. It is the process by which we steer our families, organizations, and communities toward self-rule. In doing so, we are led to partner with others through dialogue to obtain what we need for our individual and collective welfare but cannot obtain on our own. It is the essence of democracy.

Community is found in the collective expression of individual values and practices.

This book provides the reader with both the concept and practice of self-governance in communities and families. In the first section of the book, a context for successful self-governance is established. In the second, a practical dialogue tool for catalyzing and supporting self-governance in communities and families is presented. In the third section, tips and suggestions for supporting the growing historical shift to self-governance and self-rule are provided.

Coming of Age

Coming to a philosophy of self-governance and understanding its implications for communities and families has been for me a developmental journey. A brief description of that journey may help the reader to understand my approach to self-governance and the biases that underlie it. I came of age in the turbulent 1960s. I grew up in the small town of Boise, Idaho, at the foot of the Rocky Mountains. My father was a carpenter. My mother worked in my elementary school cafeteria. While growing up, I learned the value of hard work and responsibility. Neither of my parents completed college, but they taught me the importance of education. They also taught me to question authority and prize freedom and independence.

When I was young, I too thought I could change the world. And, in part, I and my generation did. While at the University of Oregon, I protested the Vietnam War in the late 1960s. After graduating from the university, I left the green of Oregon to join the War on Poverty, moving in the gray of winter to the urban landscape of Hyde Park on the south side of Chicago. There I worked as a VISTA volunteer in the Woodlawn and Englewood neighborhoods, two communities wracked by poverty and violence. I served as a paralegal for a poverty law group called the Community Legal Council and a grassroots organization, the Chicago Welfare Rights Organization. With other fresh-faced VISTA volunteers I joined a staff of only slightly older lawyers. We used the law and community action to secure the rights of poor and working people to housing, health care, and social services.

We were intent on challenging and opening up the system. We were intent on making government responsive. We were ardent advocates for the poor and working Americans and were successful in guaranteeing their social and political rights through class-action lawsuits and protest. We believed that rights and entitlements were not an end in themselves but rather a means for improving the lives of those living outside the American dream and helping them to secure that dream. We were young firebrands bent on making the dream more inclusive.

Following those early years, I went on to earn graduate degrees in social welfare from the University of California at Berkeley. After graduating, I continued to work as an advocate for disadvantaged and working people. As an academic, planner, and policy analyst I worked and taught in the San Francisco Bay Area, Idaho, and Hawaii before settling into a faculty position at the University of North Carolina at Chapel Hill.

Self-governance is the decision-making process by which we steer ourselves toward self-rule.

In the two and a half decades since my time on the southside streets of Chicago, some things have improved, others are worse. Millions of Americans who were once outside the mainstream have gained access to important social and political rights. More younger and older Americans now have access to basic health care and social services than they did before the 1960s. Children with special needs have access to mainstream public education where they did not before. Yet, for many other Americans, the burgeoning social welfare industry and expanded social and political rights have not resulted in greater self-sufficiency and freedom. For many individuals, social welfare benefits became an end rather than a means to greater self-reliance. For many, those benefits have not broken the cycle of dependence and dreams denied.

Dramatic increases in spending for social services, education, and health care have not produced commensurate results. In fact, increased spending has led to greater and greater fragmentation and confusion within the system. More children than ever are in poverty, public schools remain below par, youth violence persists, and the numbers of families and individuals without health care continue to swell.

It is clear, not just to the public but also to me and many of my colleagues in the social welfare enterprise, that our traditional approaches to management and change in the public sector do not produce the desired results. Traditional public systems are not working. It is equally clear that a purely private approach does not hold the answer. Individuals in democratic societies are first and foremost citizens, not consumers. They have a right to expect decent service from their government. Not all relationships can or should be turned into economic relationships in which the sole arbiter is private money. As a nation we are at a crossroads. Federal and state officials, policy analysts, and communities by themselves do not have the answers to our complex social problems. We are in a period of enormous flux, uncertainty, and experimentation. The public does not know whom to trust or turn to for help so public support for social spending declines, and the well-being of families and children continues to erode.

> It is clear that traditional approaches to management and change are not working.

Action Based on Self-Reflection

Our times call for action based on critical self-reflection. At this point in my life and career, I find myself experiencing much of the same self-doubt that pervades the public's perspective on government and social action. As an Associate Director for Program Development and Training at the Jordan Institute for Families at the University of North Carolina, I find myself increasingly skepti-

cal and critical of traditional approaches and assumptions underlying public interventions.

Socrates said that our youth is spent looking to the future and at
midlife we look both back to where we have been and forward to where we might go. Perhaps because I am a baby
boomer in midlife, I find myself both looking back on what
has and has not worked and turning a critical eye and ear to
seeing and hearing new and better ways to serve communities and families. Perhaps it is because I and many of my
compatriots are of the generation now in power that I find
it neither acceptable nor plausible to blame our social problems on
an anonymous system.

> Our times call
> for action based
> on critical
> self-reflection.

Because now many of us are in fact the system, it is more appropriate to reflect on our own personal and professional assumptions
about power, empowerment, and social change. It is appropriate
for us—bureaucrats, policy analysts, academics, and citizens—to
think about how we, individually and collectively, must change so
that communities and families can do better. Part of this process of
self-reflection has led me to see that many of our actions in the
public sector are at odds with our own stated intents and values.
Increasingly, I have witnessed that I and many people I respect and
admire often profess one thing and do another. As Argyis (1990)
noted, the theory we use—our actual behavior—is frequently at
odds with the theory and values we espouse. We often know better
than we do.

Let me illustrate, using a few conversations with policy colleagues and administrators that resulted in a series of epiphanies
and led me to question some of my fundamental assumptions
about social change. All the individuals in these stories profess
commitment to empowering communities and families to govern
themselves and make their own choices. Yet many of their behaviors undermine that commitment.

A number of years back, I was working with a department of state
government that was responsible for overseeing services to older
adults and people with disabilities. Because this department had no

mission statement by which to steer itself, my colleagues and I agreed to construct one. The state employees expressed a good deal of enthusiasm for the undertaking. Within a couple days, I was summoned to meet with the department manager. After greeting me pleasantly and seating me in the chair in front of her desk, she leaned across and said, "I hear that you have my people working on a mission statement. I want you to understand something about how things work in this department. I do the thinking around here. I want you to stop this activity."

On another occasion, I was working with several colleagues and state-level administrators on a multimillion-dollar effort to reform the state's complex child welfare system. A major tenet of that reform involved collaborative approaches to redesigning the system. Collaboration, everyone agreed, was essential for success. The system was too fragmented. Everyone needed to pull together. We devised a dynamic planning process that pulled the community together to strengthen families. The process would identify what worked, what did not, and initiate a redesigning of the broadly defined child welfare system. In a subsequent meeting with senior administrators, I suggested that we convene the same cross-section of players at the state level to support the process of collaboration and system redesign among the counties. A key administrator tersely dismissed the suggestion and said, "We will keep the process at the county level. It is not necessary here."

A year later, I was talking with a middle manager with the state's Work First welfare reform effort. Child welfare and Work First programs deal with many of the same families. The manager's office was two floors above the section responsible for child welfare services. In the conversation, I mentioned what was being done in the area of child welfare reform. She said she had never heard of the initiative. Collaboration had not occurred at the state level. Department-level managers frequently fail to see the connection between behaviors in one level of government and behaviors and results in other.

One last story: Not long ago I was contracting to do some policy work with two different divisions of state government with overlapping jurisdictions. Although these divisions worked fairly well together in the community, at the state level they treated each other as competitors. One day I suggested to the division director of one of the agencies that, given the past difficulties between the two systems, we should bring them together to dialogue and work those differences out. She was a rather diminutive person, but only in height. She hiked herself up in my face and said—very clearly and somewhat loudly—"No! We are not going to do that!"

These three stories and countless others like them illustrate several points. Bureaucracies tend to be top-down, command-and-control systems characterized by fragmentation, competition, and an absence of meaningful collaboration and dialogue. That is the obvious point. Less obvious is the answer to the questions, How can people who otherwise profess progressive values of empowerment and self-governance for their clients, consumers, or students behave in such decidedly undemocratic ways with their own staff and organizations? How can welfare case workers, teachers, juvenile justice, and child care workers effectively impart values of responsibility, choice, and self-sufficiency when they themselves are disempowered? The answer is that in great part they cannot.

Self-Governance and Leading by Example

All the individuals mentioned above, myself included, know better than we do. In this sense, and perhaps it is obvious, bureaucrats, educators, policy analysts, and community activists are not very different from business people, church officials, or parents. Each of us knows better and most of us are looking for better ways to match our behaviors to our values.

Part of the answer to our personal and professional challenges may lie in what the Anglican bishop learned only on his deathbed: Self-governance and learning and creative responses to change are best taught by matching words with behavior and leading by example. It may be that one of the biggest barriers to effective social action is no longer *them* but *us*. The collective us includes, first and foremost, administrators and managers in bureaucratic public sector organizations, but it also includes educators, community advocates, parents, and everyone else.

I have come to realize that we need a different approach to understanding and addressing our social problems. This book presents that approach: a new partnership between government and its citizens, a new sharing of power, a new collaboration. Using as models the experimentation in state and local governments, this book presents both framework and principles and a powerful tool—community dialogues—for nourishing self-governance.

It is certainly true, as Schorr (1997) observed that government and bureaucrats get in the way of their own purposes with their rules, regulations, and top-down, command-and-control approaches. It is equally true that ordinary citizens get in the way of securing their own purposes by shunting complex personal responsibilities onto overburdened public systems. Everyone must be prepared to change if our outcomes for families are to change. To democratize our social institutions and communities—our public selves—we must be willing to model increased self-governance in both our public and private lives. Private choices are reflected in public behaviors, and public choices are reflected in private behaviors. Our public and private lives are intertwined.

In the same manner that I reflect on my behavior as a policy analyst, planner, and educator, I find myself reflecting on my behavior as a father, a husband, and a neighbor. I am trying to listen more and value and make time for relationships that are important to me. I know that, if I and others can model self-governance in our private lives, it will make the tasks of government and our social institutions easier. I also know that, until one values oneself and family, one cannot value social institutions—schools, police, or health and human services systems. Communities and families in partnership with one another and with social institutions are responsible and capable of creating self-governing communities. Working together, we can restore trust in

To fully democratize our social institutions and communities we must model increased self-governance in our public and private lives.

our social institutions and families. Together we are instruments for order and well-being in a democratic society.

Organization of the Book

By necessity, a book appears in a linear fashion. But in fact, this book's three sections are complementary. Those of you who are more interested in practical matters may want to start with section two, which presents a dialogue tool for engaging communities and strengthening families. Section three contains tips for maintaining and deepening the momentum toward change and greater self-governance. Later, you may want to turn to the more philosophic chapters in section one that address concepts of self-governance. Each chapter and section of the book, regardless of the order in which you read it, corresponds to a component of community, organizational, and family capacity that must be built simultaneously to achieve a synergy that transforms the whole.

Section one, The Opening Up of Our Social Institutions, presents a picture of greater self-governance through partnership and dialogue. Chapter 1 sets a framework for thinking about self-governance in the management of our social institutions. Chapter 2 describes the relationships, structures, and principles of self-governance that are emerging across the country. Chapter 3 discusses the role of dialogue in forging community partnerships for strengthening families.

Section two, Community Dialogues—The Path to Self-Governance, provides an accessible approach to facilitating dialogues that enlist citizens and social institutions in collaborative problem solving. These dialogues are employed, by representatives of public and private institutions as well as by individual citizens, to obtain specific results. They show how citizens and nonprofit and government bodies can use dialogue to move toward greater self-governance. To continue the analogy, open and participatory dialogues (and democratic processes in general) are like a swiftly flowing river. Once you step in, you can never predict exactly

where you will come out. Participation requires trust in the belief
that, when individuals hold onto to one another, they can create
a bridge to get to the other side. In the process of creating that
bridge, they begin to build new relationships, structures, values,
and a sense of community that will help sustain them in the
future. Chapter 4 provides a framework and process for stepping
into the river and moving safely to the other side. It describes how
dialogue can engage the public's common purposes and moral
voice to help close the gap between dreams and actual behavior
and results. Chapters 5, 6, and 7 provide a day-by-day account of
the unfolding and uncovering of the community's voice. The
appendixes provide additional detail for settting up and running
self-governance dialogues.

In section three, Democratizing Social Governance and
Management, critical sets of issues that must be addressed if the
momentum achieved in the community dialogues is to continue
are identified. Principles and values for renorming our social
institutions are presented. Tips are provided for enhanced self-
governance. Self-governance dialogues are a catalyst for change,
not a panacea—true success is found in the follow-through.
Chapter 8 discusses the placing of shared learning and accountability into social institutions. It provides tips for supporting a
process of continous learning and adaptation. Chapter 9 identifies
our capacity for shared ownership and control of decisions and
their consequences. It provides tips for strengthening that capacity
in our social institutions. Chapter 10 discusses an all-encompass-
ing culture of self-governance. Here the values that underpin the
concept at the family, organizational, and community level are
explored in depth. Principles and practical tips are provided for
creating and maintaining a culture of self-governance. Chapters 8,
9, and 10 represent our challenge to engage the public in the governance and support of its social institutions.

This book is intended to speak to a broad audience. For many of
us—individuals inside and outside formal social institutions—the
strengthening of our families and communities is our primary pur-

pose. The book provides us with a way of thinking and with tools for reconnecting to our values, to one another, to our institutions and to a higher purpose. The issue of governance', the manner and methods by which we take decisions to strengthen our families and communities, is at the heart of a democratic civil society.

This book is not a cure for the ills our society. It does not directly address such issues as race, gender, inequality, and poverty. It is not issue oriented, but process oriented, addressing the process of self-governance as facilitated by dialogue and open communication.

The book is optimistic in outlook. It presumes that, when given enough information and held accountable for our choices, most of us will make wise decisions about our lives, families, and communities. But we must also recognize that the practice of self-governance has its limitations. Not all people are ready to govern themselves, exercise choice, and behave responsibly. Not all people are prepared to be both free and responsible. There are mistakes and failures in the practice of self-governance. But I have rarely if ever met an individual, family, organization, or community that doesn't aspire to greater self-governance.

This book draws on many voices, stories, and metaphors to illustrate the overarching themes and assumptions behind the emerging philosophy of self-governance and self-management. It may be considered a conversation about our common future and our individual and collective rights and responsibilities. I hope that you, the reader, will find it thought provoking, informative, and useful.

The Opening Up of Our Social Institutions

The landscape of our social institutions and programs is shifting. Cracks are appearing in the traditional approaches to the governance and management of human services, education, and health care. The values and assumptions that in the past have given form to these institutions and their management are being challenged. Our social institutions and programs are beginning to open up and transform themselves.

Through these cracks and openings and the process of transformation, we are seeing the early edge of an emergence of more open and democratic institutions and programs. They are characterized by public and private partnerships, a focus on results, and a reassertion of the citizens' ownership and responsibility for the welfare of family and community. This opening up presents an opportunity for the further engagement of the public in the redesign of its social institutions and programs through a process of reflection and dialogue. Greater reflection and dialogue around a common purpose will serve to deepen the public's commitment to its social institutions and to the families and communities served by those institutions.

CHAPTER I

Creating a Framework for Self-Governance

COMMUNITY VOICES: The clouds were much darker and heavier than usual. The air was strangely still. You could smell the ocean. I knew that Hurricane Fran would come ashore that evening somewhere near Wilmington, North Carolina. This was no fall thunderstorm. Yet I wanted to believe that hurricanes, like many forms of chaos and violence, happened somewhere else and to someone else. I was sure that we would be safe in Raleigh, more than a hundred miles inland.

Around two o'clock that morning, we were awakened by flashes of lightning coming through our bedroom windows and by ear-splitting peals of thunder. Nearby, we heard one tree fall and then another. We went upstairs, gathered up the sleeping children, and brought them to our room. No sooner were we settled than the lights flickered and went out. The house went dark. The wind howled. A moment later the house shook as a tree crashed against it. We found a candle, lit it, and moved the children down into the basement. We burrowed deeper into our home for safety.

As we entered the basement we heard running water. It wasn't outside. It was pouring out of the ceiling vents and splashing onto the floor. We moved our children onto a pull-out couch in the basement den. My wife and I placed large buckets under the vents to capture the rain. They were emptied and replaced many times during the early hours of the morning. In a neighborhood without light, in a house without light, you feel alone.

The early morning sunbeams streamed through the white oaks and loblolly pine. I looked out and listened. The leaves and needles glistened and dripped with the remnants of the night's torrential rains. I heard faint but welcome voices in the neighborhood. Adults and children began to emerge from their homes in my suburban cul-de-sac.

I joined them. We flowed together as a unified band and toured our neighborhood. Together, we observed that a large pine had blown across the community's only exit, a neighbor's car had been crushed in his driveway, and a tall, slim sweetgum had, like a guillotine, sheared the gutters and porch lights off a neighbor's home, coming to rest against the full length of the house. We asked each person who joined the band if anyone were hurt or if their property were damaged. We asked neighbors what kind of help they needed. And we asked for help.

A Community Responds

On an early September night, Hurricane Fran ripped across the North Carolina coast. It plowed up the Cape Fear River with one hundred-mile-an-hour winds, tornadoes, and microbursts, bringing death, destruction, and flooding a hundred miles inland. Twenty-one people died in North Carolina. More than $5 billion in storm-related damage was sustained. More than a million people lost power for days.

Yet, in the minutes and hours after the storm and with no prior planning, North Carolina citizens went to work. They joined family, friends, strangers, and public and private agencies, including private utility crews from as far away as Florida, to assist one another, clear roads, secure homes, and reestablish power.

The timing of Hurricane Fran was uncanny. On the evening of the hurricane, the University of North Carolina at Chapel Hill was holding a seminar on the demise of community in America. The conference had to be canceled as citizens and students came together in unprecedented numbers to assist one another. The response to the disruption of a hurricane revealed a tremendous intrinsic capacity for self-organization and regeneration in the face of chaos. Public, private, and individual resources were tapped to begin the process of rebuilding immediately. Normal bureaucratic barriers and procedures were put aside to get the job done. The circle of mutual assistance was extended beyond the usual reach of public and voluntary organizations to engage the broader capacity of citizens at large. Through actions small and large, people of goodwill in both the public and private sectors lent a hand to their fellow citizens. Communities were united in the feeling that we were all in this together.

Social Chaos

Society also has it hurricanes. Jonesboro, Arkansas, is a small mainstream southern town. On a spring day, eleven-year-old Drew Golden and thirteen-year-old Mitch Johnson were alleged to have lured their schoolmates and teachers into a schoolyard with a false fire alarm and then methodically killed four young girls and a teacher. The incident made the front pages and headlines all across the country. A community and nation were stunned by the senseless violence. In the days after the tragedy, parents in this rural corner of America experienced a palpable fear for their children's safety when they left for school each day. Parents all across the nation gave pause for their children's security.

Society has its hurricanes born of many small untended responsibilities

Far away in Springfield, Massachusetts, in the poor, predominantly minority McKnight neighborhood, five women were murdered. No suspects were identified. There was no national outrage or press coverage; the local media even dismissively referred to one of the young women as a crack addict. The associate director of the Girls Center there tells of being unable to walk the few blocks from the center to her mother's home in the evening. She is afraid. She tells stories of parents unable to let their children play in public playgrounds even during the day because of the threat of drugs and violence. She grew up in the neighborhood. It was not always like this; it had once been a strong and safe neighborhood.

The incidents are different and yet the residents of both the McKnight and Jonesboro communities—neighbors, parents, grandparents, and children—were experiencing similar feelings. They were concerned for their families and their children, and they felt powerless. Jonesboro and Springfield are not unlike thousands of places big and small across the nation. In recent decades, destructive social problems have grown like weeds and spread from countless seeds of neglect and unattended responsibility. In towns such as Jonesboro, Arkansas, these social problems seem to spring up unexpectedly. In neighborhoods like McKnight in Springfield, Massachusetts, footholds have been established and social problems are pervasive.

Young children across the nation are going unsupervised and without effective adult role models. Inadequate parental supervision, substance abuse, child abuse and neglect, and even the lack of books in the home all are factors that contribute to long-term damaging consequences for children, families, and society. These initial risk factors are society's red flags. Unless they are prevented or responded to effectively, they will continue to snowball into lifetimes of failure for both the affected individuals and their communities.

Self-Governance and Self-Organization

We must redesign our social insitutions and widen our personal circles of mutal assistance to one another.

The primary message of this book is that it need not be this way. Communities, poor and mainstream, have an inherent capacity to respond effectively to natural and artificial disasters. Like natural disasters, chaotic social conditions such as youth violence and family disruption can generate powerful self-organizing and adaptive responses. We as citizens and members of families have the capacity to organize and reassert order. But to tap this capacity, we must acknowledge that the traditional way of dealing with social problems has not worked and that a purely voluntary or private-sector approach is not feasible. Instead, we must join public and private institutions in taking responsibility for our collective and individual actions. We must redesign our social institutions and widen our personal circles of mutual assistance to one another.

This book presents a structure and philosophy by which to manage and govern social programs and a practical dialogue tool to help local communities build their capacity for self-governance. It goes beyond either/or notions of public versus private approaches to see with a third eye a vision of collaboration and partnership between public and private institutions. It uses dialogue to help us see, hear, and create a different future.

All across the country, citizens are hard at work redesigning public and private institutions to serve families more effectively. Social institutions are opening up and changing. This book connects the dots of these successful innovations into a comprehensive vision and map for increasingly self-governing communities and families. People in different parts of the country, working separately from one another in a trial-and-error manner, have developed different approaches that do work. This book pulls these various approaches together into a comprehensive outline that can be communicated to others. It builds on the work of Bruner, Both, and Marzke (1996), Osborne and Plastrik (1997), Schorr (1997), and many others in constructing that vision.

Public institutions are opening up through a process of decentralization and greater citizen participation. The current historic devolution of power and responsibility from federal to state and local government creates an opportunity to replace top-down governance with more bottom-up and inside-out self-governance at all levels. Such a devolution in power and decision making creates an opportunity for meaningful dialogue between citizens and their institutions. When the public becomes more engaged, public and private institutions become stronger, more effective, and better able to serve families and children. That is the essence of democracy.

At its heart, this book is about ourselves. The failure of our social institutions to hold themselves accountable for results parallels our private failure as a culture to hold ourselves accountable for our behaviors and the well-being of our families and children. The concepts of social regeneration and self-governance apply to our social institutions, our workplaces, our neighborhoods, and our personal lives.

Restoring Trust in Public Institutions

Trust in government has eroded over the past several decades. The public believes that public institutions alone cannot solve the complex social problems facing families. Much of the public also believes that individual citizens and private associations by themselves are not equal to the task. What is apparent to more and more of us is that *working together* holds our only chance for success.

Society's response to natural and artificial disasters illustrates that we can collaborate and work together effectively when we decide to. At such times, we transcend the limitations of bureaucracies and formal roles and status to take advantage of what each of us personally can contribute to solve the problem. We rebuild after Hurricane Fran. We come together for a period of mourning and reflection in Jonesboro. We are able to take advantage, at least temporarily, of the relationships in the community that are necessary to respond to the task at hand. The challenge for us all is to sustain collaboration and partnerships over time. Meeting this challenge and in the process restoring public trust in social institutions requires that we change the way we keep track of what is important: our relationships with one another, our results, and our ownership of the process.

Working together holds our only chance of success.

A self-governing society combines the strengths of both the traditional public and private sectors. It creates a third perspective on social governance and decision making. An overview of the traditional approaches to relationships, results, and ownership demonstrates that a new alternative is needed. It helps us to think about and construct that alternative. A new alternative that creates both structures and a culture of enhanced self-governance makes the management of social programs more democratic.

RELATIONSHIPS

Susan is a child with developmental needs, growing up in California. By the time she was eight years old, she had had six different doctors, five nurses, six case managers, three therapists, and seven teachers. With the involvement of several well-meaning but uncoordinated and overlapping agencies and professionals, the quality of care and the family's sense of control are undermined.

In the traditional public sector, planners break the problems of families and individuals into finer and finer segments. A categorical program with separate eligibility guidelines is created for each segment of the problem. A complex series of bureaucratic monopolies determines which services an individual will receive and where and when. Relationships within such a system are complex and fragmented. Bureaucracies segment work. Uncomfortable with collaboration and partnership, bureaucracies fail to integrate work and relationships. That discomfort fragments what should be a unified web of support and accountability.

In the private for-profit sector, relationships are driven by competition and private resources. Competition is seen as the engine that creates both choice and efficiency. But the family with a child who is developmentally delayed often has multiple needs for specialized tutoring, counseling, respite, and medical treatment. For such families, competition frequently undermines the collaborative multipronged approach that is necessary to produce useful results.

A third approach that ensures greater efficiency and effectiveness is possible. In self-governing communities, cooperation and collaboration drive creative problem solving and produce results. Competition in the public sector is not, in fact, in short supply. Battles over organizational turf are legion and constitute some of the biggest barriers to learning and innovation. What is in short supply is cooperative and collaborative models that foster diverse approaches to problem solving and recognize that everyone's contribution is needed. Many states are experimenting with building collaborative family support and prevention partnerships. In Florida, the approach is called TEAM Florida. It is a process whereby the community works as a team with the family. The contributions of various parts of the community are blended and synchronized, and families are supported in a way that efficiently shares resources and honors choice. In this postentitlement era, the

new safety net is the web of public and private relationships dedicated to the well-being of families and children.

RESULTS

The Illinois Department of Public Welfare tracks precisely how
many clients it has served, at what cost, and with what combination of services. Over the past decade, its budget has climbed
more than fourfold, from $350 million to more than $1.2 billion.
Paradoxically, while the department's spending has increased, the
number of children removed from families and placed in foster
care has also increased from around fifteen thousand to more
than forty thousand. Only recently has the department begun to
examine results for families associated with its social spending.
Historically, the bottom line for many public institutions has been
"services delivered" and "money spent." Public institutions have
been in the business of meeting the citizen's perceived service
needs with the assumption that well-intentioned services would
lead to good results. The evidence indicates that this is not always
the case.

In contrast, the barometer of success in the private sector is
profit, not consumers served or money invested. Profit-driven
approaches to social governance and accountability are attractive
to many in government whether the subject is building prisons or
finding jobs for welfare recipients. Profit is seen as providing a
bottom-line measure in evaluating the effectiveness of decisions
and a discipline that is missing in traditional public programs.

But for self-governing communities and institutions, the critical
measure of success is "valued results" for families and children.
Financial profits can be made from nursing homes and foster care
for children, but that result is not valued by most of the families,
elderly citizens, or children involved. For families profit is the provision of appropriate and loving care to those who need it.
Providing elderly citizens with the option of continuing to live at
home or securing a permanent family for children for example, are

valued results. Citizens are capable of deciding how much they are willing to spend for results they value.

OWNERSHIP

In Wisconsin, the mother of a child arrested for car theft expresses a typical feeling of disempowerment upon entering the juvenile justice system: "When we entered the court, everyone was already there. The judge began to list what 'we' were going to do for Robert. I began to wonder whose kid this was anyway."

In many traditional public systems, whether the discussion concerns juvenile justice, child welfare, or the schools, the *system* owns both the relationships and the results associated with the clients or students who fall within its jurisdiction. The schools are responsible for educational results and for the values and behaviors of students. Public welfare agencies are responsible for results such as the mitigation of abuse and neglect and movement from welfare to work. The juvenile justice system is responsible for adolescent offenders and for juvenile crime.

In comparison, ownership of results in the private sector is private. Both the relationships and the results are owned by private companies and corporations. Private ownership and the clear bottom line of profit and return on investment are seen as contributing to both efficiency and effectiveness. Private ownership is seen as creating a self-interest that provides the motivation for quality performance.

In a democratic society, however, ownership and responsibility for results are more complex. Families are the primary owners of their relationships and results. When families are self-governing, they direct their own relationships. They direct their learning and adaptation. They are responsible for their own well-being. Self-governing families require less governance from external agents either public or private. They take responsibility for themselves. When public and private associations are implemented, they serve as instruments for bringing about desired results in partnership with families.

FIGURE 1: **Shift in Social Governance and Decision-Making**

	TRADITIONAL PERSPECTIVES		SELF-GOVERNANCE
	PUBLIC	PRIVATE	PUBLIC AND PRIVATE TOGETHER
Relationships	Control	Competition	Collaborative Partnerships
Results	Service	Profit	Results at Reasonable Costs
Ownership	System	Private Owners	Communities and Families

Traditional public- and private-sector approaches to governance have both merits and shortcomings. Self-governance marks a third way that combines the best of the two approaches and creates something more. In self-governing communities and families, the focus is on collaborative, in contrast to competitive or control-oriented relationships; valued results for families, not just profit or services; and community and family ownership rather than private or system ownership of results. Figure 1 captures the shift in social governance and decision making for social programs.

Managing Social Programs More Democratically

Improving results for the nation's families will not be accomplished by importing the newest management fad into the public sector. Downsizing the public sector, doing more with less, privatizing public functions, increasing service integration, or expanding the role of the private nonprofit charitable sector will not guarantee more efficient or effective services. None of these strategies changes the basic structure and culture of the dominant social institutions, and none of them addresses the connection between powerful systems and disempowered citizens.

Valued results can be achieved by opening up social institutions and creating a culture of partnership between those institutions and their citizens. In this partnership, both administrators and ordinary citizens create a reflective and self-correcting process. It is an approach that enhances self-governance at all levels of society. Self-governance as described in this book is a process in which we make decisions, form relationships, and take responsibility for our own behavior and results. It is a process in which we partner with others to achieve what we cannot accomplish on our own. It is a positive cyclic process in which assistance from others generates a desire to reciprocate in kind when the need arises. Self-governance is characterized by a capacity for self-organization and self-evaluation. We direct our own learning and maximize our own well-being through continuous reflection and adaptation. The process is similar at the individual, family, organizational, and community levels. It is a paradoxical approach to change that moves from the inside out and in the process links individuals to families and families to a web of caring and supportive public and private relationships. It is an approach that creates an enhanced sense of community and collective efficacy.

> Self-governance is the process by which we partner with others to achieve what we cannot accomplish on our own.

The belief that common purposes can be achieved through enhanced self-governance is derived from a basic respect for the goodness and talent of public and private servants and ordinary citizens. Change is fueled by tapping people's desire to contribute something of value to their families and children and community. When these talents and diverse perspectives are pooled into problem-solving networks and teams, they hold the greatest promise of turning back the tide of poor results.

When we engage the voices of all those who have a stake in improving results, we create a collective sense of common purpose. We set our moral compass. Families increase their responsibility for themselves when they have a say in and authority over how those responsibilities are to be met. Engaging the voices of all those interested in the well-being of families changes the nature of social decision making, making it democratic.

Government's role in a democratic society increasingly involves fostering inclusive and collaborative relationships, helping to create and share information on valued results at the community level, and fostering the citizens' ownership of democratic processes and results. Without participation and collaboration, citizens cannot take an active role in crafting and implementing new strategies to secure common purposes. Without information on results, the public cannot know whether communities and families are achieving their common purposes. But with open and collaborative participation, accountability for results, and a democratic ownership of those results, order and well-being among the nation's families and children is within reach.

Public Management as Dialogue and Collaboration

The way we "know and understand life" shapes the way we live our lives. Our science, culture, and correspondingly, our notions of management are moving away from machine metaphors of knowing and understanding communities, organizations, and families toward more holistic and dynamic models. If we think of social organization as a machine, each of us—as individuals or as members of families, organizations, and communities—is but a removable part in a hierarchic structure, an independent, replaceable, and expendable cog in a wheel. The act and process of knowing one another is impersonal and objective. We are distanced from one another. The captains of our slow-moving impersonal systems command our allegiance and provide us with direction (Ellinor and Gerard 1998). We don't take full responsibility for either ourselves or our social institutions.

> To understand individuals is to understand their capacity and need for relatedness to others—family and community.

In the models of social institutions that we are moving toward, each part contains the whole and the whole in turn is made up of unique parts. Every part of the family has an image of the whole and his or her contribution to its vitality and adaptability. Each part contributes to the well-being of each child in its midst. Those contributions or their absence are reflected in the life of each child. To understand individuals is to understand their capacity and need for relatedness to others—family and community. To understand individuals is to understand their personal, cultural, and spiritual history (Palmer, 1990).

With this shift in perspective, our view of management and change in large social institutions also shifts. Leaders serve as stewards and facilitators of self-organizing and self-governing systems centered around an evolving sense of common purpose and identity. Direction is achieved through a confluence of inputs from all parts of the community. Information moves openly, freely, and rapidly to all parts. Each of us—community leader, bureaucrat, teacher, student, and citizen—must be able to reference what the others are doing so that everyone can adjust successfully to changing conditions.

> Dialogue is the process by which we breathe new life into our relationships and into ourselves.
>
> LINDA ELLINOR & GLENNA GERARD

Dialogue is the medium through which information is communicated and moved around and self-referencing occurs. Dialogue is the lens through which we see our connection to the whole. It is how we identify, share, and periodically adapt our mental models of the world. It is through dialogue that we build and sustain a culture of collaborative problem solving. In an increasingly integrated world, effective communication is more important than ever. Danah Zohar (1997) observes that the word *dialogue* has two complementary translations. The recent translation of the Greek words *dia* and *logos is* "through (*dia*) words (*logos*)." The earlier and more original translation of *logos* is " relationship." Dialogue, in this translation, means through relationships.

In thinking about the public and private management of self, dialogue is a process by which we breathe new life into our relationships and into ourselves through those relationships (Ellinor and Gerard 1998). Through words and relationships, public managers and citizens inquire with others into the assumptions behind their actions. They see the whole among all the parts and the connections between those parts; they create a structure and culture that fosters continuous learning through inquiry and self-referencing; and they help to identify the common purposes and motivation necessary to adapt in a changing environment.

To manage and solve problems within communities, organizations, and families successfully, we must attend to our relationships, build trust and an underlying respect for what each contributes, and blend those relationships and contributions to achieve valued results for our families and children. To understand the paradox of self-governance is to appreciate the connection among the individual self, the family, and the larger community. We find such an understanding by respecting the desire of each part of the whole to manage and govern itself in partnership with others.

A New Movement

In a national gathering on parenting, David Harris of the MacArthur Foundation commented on a conversation he had with Ossie Davis, an important figure in the Civil Rights movement. Lamenting the fact that he had missed the opportunity to participate in the Civil Rights movement of the 1950s and 1960s, not being of that generation, Harris asked when Davis foresaw the next great social movement coming about. Davis said, "You know, there are people all over this country doing great things. They have their noses to the ground. They are working hard helping people and communities achieve a better life. They are doing many great things. The next great movement for social progress will come about when all these people look up and join hands and voices in common cause."

CHAPTER 2

Opening Up Our Social Institutions

COMMUNITY VOICES: Velma shuffled her feet nervously as she waited her turn. She was wondering why she had agreed to do this. She dreaded getting up in front of a lot of people she didn't know, especially government people. Would they listen to an old black grandma like herself?

It had been just three months since she received a late night call from her eldest daughter, but it seemed so much longer. Two years ago, running from a bad situation into the unknown, Vanessa had moved to California from Florida with her four children. Just before she left Florida, her latest boyfriend left her. He grew tired of drying her out only to have her fall back into repeated bouts of alcohol and pills. She took the children and left. Now the state was going to take Vanessa's children and place them in foster care. Her daughter pleaded with Velma to do something. What could she do? A retired widow, she could barely provide for herself. But she couldn't let her grandchildren go to strangers. She had to do something. She took in her four grandchildren. The oldest was only twelve.

But taking them in was not the hardest part. She went back to work as a cashier at a local supermarket, but still did not have enough money for clothes and shoes, and school was ready to start. She finally gave in and called the social services folks to ask for a little help until she could get on her feet. Tears came to her eyes as she recalled how she had been questioned. Did she have any savings? How much money did she make? Why couldn't her daughter take care of her own children? Was she really fit to take care of four little children? Then, after all that, they said she was not eligible for any help. She was passed onto another agency, and the questions started all over again. She felt humiliated.

A voice called her name. Startled, she looked up. She dried her eyes with the back of her hand. It was her turn to speak to the community gathering. This was the first time anyone had ever asked her opinion on how things could be improved in her community. Maybe they would listen. Maybe they would do something to improve the way people were treated when they needed a helping hand. She was hopeful.

Good Enough for Government Work

Many have come to believe that government and public services cannot be compassionate or directly responsive to citizens such as Velma. Government and public bureaucracies have been in disrepute for so many years now that it is hard to remember past successes. It is hard to imagine that things could be different. Distrust and suspicion of government run deep. Just as "made in Japan" has come to represent a standard of excellence, the phrase "good enough for government work" once connoted a standard of excellence in this country (Linden 1994). Not that long ago government and the public sector were seen in a more positive light.

Distrust and suspicion of government run deep.

With the New Deal in the 1930s and the creation in the 1940s and 1950s of a model secondary and postsecondary education system and a transcontinental highway network, government was seen by the public as a positive force for change and effective problem solving. Memories of these and other successes have dimmed in the past several decades as government programs and bureaucracy became more centralized, fragmented, and isolated.

A Strong Government

Alexis de Tocqueville (1990) observed years ago that it is important to make the distinction between a government that sets the broad parameters and principles by which citizens and communities govern themselves and a government that administers particular policies and measures for its people. A strong government is necessary to ensure a level and democratic playing field. When, however, government directly administers social policies, it risks undermining the inherent capacity and responsibility of citizens and communities to administer their own affairs. The test of a democratic government is its willingness to return the direct administration of public matters to the communities and citizens involved. Failure to return that responsibility results in an unwarranted concentration and centralization of power in federal and state government. In this failure, government undermines the very sense of community and well-being that it had hoped to create.

Until recently, there has been no looking back and no returning of responsibility for self-governance to local communities and families. However, in recent years, government has begun to open up and reaffirm the principles of local self-governance and individual responsibility. It has begun the process of resetting the broad parameters and principles by which citizens and communities govern themselves.

The test of a democratic government is its willingness to return the direct administration of public matters to the involved communities and its citizens.

ALEXIS DE TOCQUEVILLE

Opening Up Social Institutions

An approach to community governance and management that incorporates these broad parameters and principles can help us view our increasingly uncertain, complex, and at times frightening world in a different light. The change need not be as scary as we imagine if we view it through new lenses. A great deal will be required of all of us. The transition will not be without pain, but like a storm, that pain will pass.

By creating a partnership between different elements of the community and the family and between government and its citizens, the emerging approach to management and enhanced self-governance produces both order and greater freedom. It recognizes the natural tendency and capacity for self-governance and self-regulation that underlie our basic sense of freedom. In this new partnership, government facilitates an open, democratic approach to self-rule. Although the general destination is clear—stronger communities and healthier families—the various paths are not determined in advance. Everyone on the journey must be willing to change his or her assumptions about how best to strengthen communities and families along the way.

What will replace traditional approaches to social governance and management in the public sector is the growing ability and capacity for self-governance at all levels of society. A complex, distant, and bureaucratic approach to government and management is being replaced with new and democratic partnerships between citizens and government and a new approach and philosophy of self-governance and self-management. In these partnerships, relationships are collaborative, results refer to actual changes in family and community well-being at reasonable costs, and the ownership for both relationships and results lies with communities and families.

The new models for governance structure, management approach, and public service culture that are beginning to emerge across the country have many characteristics in common. The characteristics are like pieces of a new puzzle. As yet few, if any, communities have put together all the pieces. And unlike static puzzles and puzzle pieces, each community, while still honoring the principles that underlie each characteristic, will put the pieces together in ways that are unique and fitted to the circumstances. In each community, context will shape and color the structures and approaches that are designed to strengthen families. Among these characteristics are:

Decentralized power

Responsible citizens

Broad-based decision making

Thinking in terms of the community

Coordinated multifaceted programs

Flexible relationships

Open and quality information systems

Local control of finances
Results-oriented culture

DECENTRALIZED POWER

As the director of the state department of mental health in
Missouri in the late 1980s, Keith Shafer was concerned about social
problems eating away at system structures and draining agency
budgets (Schorr 1997). He was interested in piloting a prevention
approach that built on the strengths of families and communities
to keep problems from reaching crisis levels. He helped form a
partnership of state divisions and commissions of mental health,
education, social services, the Saint Louis Danforth Foundation,
and Saint Louis schools. This partnership led to a program of collaboration between schools and communities, the first being the
Walbridge Caring Community. Walbridge was a school located in a
poor, largely African American neighborhood in north Saint Louis.
Together with the school's principal, James Ewing, and its school
coordinator, Khatib Waheed, Shafer developed a vision of comprehensive services, neighborhood safety, and family well-being.

Because of the program's success, in 1995 the Missouri leg-
islature invested an additional $24 million in the Caring
Communities vision and expanded it to some fifty sites
statewide.

Stewardship as practiced by Keith Shafer and Khatib
Waheed encourages greater self-management and self-
governance and decreases reliance on the management
strategies of control and compliance. It returns power to citizens and the community. It puts into practice such sayings as
"It takes a village to raise a child" by creating partnerships
among government and citizens who recognize that interdependence. Partnership and interdependence replace bureaucracy
and top-down patriarchy as the avenues for improving results
(Block 1993). Stewardship recognizes that the village in its organizations and families, has the answers to difficult social problems within itself. Stewards are those elected officials, leaders, and managers

Stewards of
self-government
trust the repre-
sentatives of
the community
to teach them
how better to
achieve results.

who *trust* the representatives of the village and community *to teach* them how better to achieve positive results. Each party shares in defining a common vision, assuming a mutual responsibility for the current situation, designing a path to improved outcomes, and taking personal action to ensure the success of the overall endeavor.

Peter Block (1993) astutely observes that decentralization and the downsizing of government or a business is not necessarily accompanied by stewardship or a change in traditional practices of governance and bureaucracy. It may simply involve pushing patriarchy and bureaucracy down to another level. Even with the passage of welfare reform, states may still recreate within their own boundaries the bureaucracy and limitation of choices that previously characterized the federal government's relationship to the states. Stewardship, in contrast, involves building the social architecture, institutions, and structures to support choice and ownership at every level of society, from the federal government right down to the ordinary citizen on the street.

RESPONSIBLE CITIZENS

Patty Smith had been in an abusive relationship with her husband for years. When she finally gathered up the courage and her children and left, she fell into dire financial straits. When she applied for welfare, she told the agency that it was temporary until she could go on her own. The first few months were a real struggle. The kids needed help with school and she needed help getting a job. In her rural Wisconsin community, there were few resources. The one place she could and did turn to was Northwoods Family Resource Center. There, the staff matched her willingness to assume responsibility for herself and her family with basic support and assistance. They helped her access relationships that were essential to her family's success and well-being. The Resource Center put its mission of family and communities working together into practice.

In the traditional welfare system, receipt of public assistance and services has been an end in itself. Welfare programs were designed to provide income benefits, not jobs. Family support services and local partnership with business and civic groups that helped move individuals from welfare to work were largely unavailable. The individual's responsibility for achieving self-sufficiency was diminished. Welfare recipients were disempowered.

Self-governance, the assumption of responsibility for steering one's own fate, does not imply that only one party has control or responsibility. To the degree that welfare reform is seen as placing responsibility for economic well-being only on welfare recipients, it violates the philosophy of self-governance whereby citizens work in partnership with government. Self-governance stresses *a shared responsibility* for moving the nation's poorest citizens from welfare to work, a responsibility shared by the whole—the business and religious sectors, the public and nonprofit services sectors, and the welfare recipients themselves.

For individuals on welfare to become empowered, they must discover their own voice, make their own choices, and take responsibility for their own actions. Taking individual responsibility is at the heart of empowerment and freedom. But although it begins with the individual, responsibility extends into the community and family and government. For communities to become empowered, their business, religious, civic, and philanthropic sectors must add their voices and exercise their responsibility to assist others less fortunate. Ending welfare as we know it is both an individual and a collective responsibility.

BROAD-BASED DECISION MAKING

Together We Can is a national leadership development and capacity-building initiative designed to strengthen children, families, and communities across the nation. It is a collaborative undertaking of The Institute for Educational Leadership, California Tomorrow, the Child and Family Policy Center, and the Program for Community Problem Solving. The initiative emphasizes inclusive decision making at the community level rather than top-down planning and control from distant central offices. To this end, it promotes extensive public education, consumer and neighborhood participation, and accountability for results. It believes that success is fostered by encouraging risk taking and experimentation, changing community and organizational cultures, and building a management approach that produces learning organizations and communities.

When we emphasize everyone's contribution and responsibility for the whole, we bring into play new resources, strengths, and a diversity of perspectives on how to improve results. As communities and families search for new connections and partnerships that will yield improved results, a process of experimentation leading to improved family well-being is unleashed.

Everyone, not just experts, must be involved in the process of change—systems must be open and inclusive. Open systems continually invite participation from people in all walks of life, experiment with new approaches, and evaluate and reflect on their results; they challenge themselves to stay on their toes so that they can best serve citizens. Dynamic planning and growth is a process whereby previously isolated players and systems are engaged in an ongoing dialogue about change and growth. Planning in today's environment is a dynamic, fluid process.

THINKING IN TERMS OF THE COMMUNITY

In regions of the country as different from each other as Arapaho in rural eastern North Carolina and Boston, Massachusetts, people are creating greater school choice through charter schools and partnerships between public and private schools. What many of these choices for alternative schooling have in common is an enhanced focus on the role of communities and families in high-performing schools. Performance is not the product of a separate educational establishment or of categorical programs. It is a function of community and family responsibility in partnership with the schools.

The Arapaho Charter School is a nonprofit community-based school. It is publicly funded. The Edison School in Boston is operated by a private for-profit company, the Edison Company, and funded by both public and private resources. Both schools possesses governance

boards with enhanced community and parent participation.
Education flourishes when it is supported actively in the boardroom,
by the faith community, and at home as well as in the classroom.

Public education is invigorated by enhanced community and
parent participation. Such schools empower all parties through
more inclusive participation, experimentation with new collaborative partnerships, and increased accountability for results. The
vitality of such schools lies not in their hierarchies, functions, and
tasks but in their ability to forge new and productive relationships.
Red tape is replaced with innovative partnerships.

The ability of varied interest groups and individuals in Boston,
Massachusetts, and Arapaho, North Carolina, and elsewhere to see
their long-term interest in helping children secure a better education is a measure of their ability to recognize a common self-interest in helping others succeed. Just as self-interest motivates a business to partner with the educational community, self-interest can
motivate parents to play a more active role in the education of
their children and their neighbors' children.

COORDINATED MULTIFACETED PROGRAMS

Louisville, Kentucky, is taking a multifaceted approach to creating
family support networks. Referred to as Neighborhood Place,
Louisville's experiment involves a sweeping decentralization of
public-sector staff serving families and children. Developed originally to help community schools achieve higher graduation rates,
it teams various professionals with families and neighborhood
councils in new and more effective approaches to problem solving.

Through Neighborhood Place, teachers, nurses, social workers,
welfare workers, community police officers, and others join in a
more flexible approach that stresses finding what works rather
than relying on preexisting professional roles or service designs. A
police officer may provide outreach for a family that has experienced domestic violence. A public health nurse may join a social
worker in supporting efforts to strengthen the parenting skills of a
new mother. Rather than relying on what systems were originally

designed to do, community teams form approaches based on what works. The stewardship for Neighborhood Place is provided through a management group comprising directors and senior staff from the public agencies involved, county and city government, and the United Way. Care is taken to balance the involvement of public agencies with participation and ownership in the neighborhood and from the private sector.

This model contrasts with traditional social programs that focus on the part, not the whole, and look for single causes when problems really have interdependent, complex causes. Neither responsibility for problems nor their control lies with one or two players. Responsibility, the power and energy for change, lies with many players. Everyone shares it. Consequently, effective social programs consist, not of one intervention, but of a cluster of interventions, small and large, formal and informal. These interventions help citizens to self-organize, experiment, and grow their way to a future characterized by improved circumstances. Taken together, the contributions of the various players in the social intervention process—public agencies, business, nonprofit organizations, and the religious and spiritual community—shape the future. However, the exact nature of that future or the effect of interdependent contributions cannot be predicted in advance; credit for achieving valued results is shared by the entire community.

FLEXIBLE RELATIONSHIPS

Georgia's state-level Policy Council for Children and Families has created partnerships with its local counterparts, the Community Partnerships. The Policy Council is authorized by state statute. The governor, the lieutenant governor, and the speaker of the house appoint the council's members, who include leadership from the state's human services sector and the corporate community. This partnership between state and local agencies creates more flexible funding approaches, innovative and collaborative service strategies, partnerships between the public and private sectors, local leadership development, and local governance and accountability structures that ensure the coherent policy and accessible, responsive services that produce desired results. It supports creative state-local partnerships to deal with teen pregnancy, child abuse and neglect, and school success.

Other states and local communities are also creating flexible and responsive systems for families. Maryland, Vermont, Washington, Oregon, and Georgia are in the forefront in shaping governance compacts that outline state and local roles and responsibilities that will produce flexible strategies for families and children. Whereas traditional hierarchy has a philosophy of managing and controlling, stewardship and self-governance operate on principles of inclusive ownership and flexible problem solving. Management is driven by vision and measured against results. In a self-governing community and organization, the people form the structure, fitting and refashioning it to serve a democratically determined vision to obtain valued results. To the degree that people are in control, they are able to self-organize and self-govern (Pinchot and Pinchot 1993). To the degree that the people are in control and the structure addresses their wants, the process is democratic and responsive. In self-governing and self-organizing systems, community and organizational structures are always kept flexible and emphasize relationships, team work, and trust, not elaborate rules and procedures.

> To the degree that people are in control, they are able to self-organize and self-govern.

OPEN AND QUALITY INFORMATION SYSTEMS

Family to Family, sponsored by the Annie E. Casey Foundation, is designed to reform the nation's foster-care system by using a new type of information system. Pilot programs have been launched in Alabama, New Mexico, Ohio, and Pennsylvania.

Historically, the information used to make policy judgments about foster care has been derived from federal reporting requirements; the experiences of children on a given day are assumed to describe the experiences of all children in foster care. Unfortunately, such caseload profiles are biased toward the experience of children and families who have the longest stays and poorest experiences in foster care. Because the profiles do not capture successful experiences in the system, they create the perception that most children drift in foster care, moving from placement to placement. Such information creates a sense that the public sector is both powerless and futile and erodes the confidence of the public and the child welfare system itself.

> Information is our lifeblood— it defines who we are, what we are doing, and how successful we are at doing it.

Information is the life-blood of an empowered community. Structures, beliefs, values, power, and purpose are expressed through information. In a complex and dynamic system, information about the results of actions is constantly fed back into the system and merged with new information in a process that ensures continuing creativity and change. Information gives order to chaos by defining who we are, what we are doing, and how successful we are. By building historical data sets that capture the actual experience of children and families over time, Family to Family enables state and local communities to identify children who are experiencing extended stays or disruptions in care and to focus attention where the problems persist.

Meg Wheatley (1992) uses the metaphor of a salmon when talking about information. In communities and organizations where the streams are well stocked, information finds its way to where it is needed. A central task of stewardship is to ensure that the streams are clear so that salmon have an easy time getting to where they need to go. Categorical programs and hierarchical bureaucracies are like dams. It is expensive to get the salmon over and around them. When the streams are kept open, when the information is allowed to flow freely, the result is a harvest of new strategies and improved results.

LOCAL CONTROL OF FINANCES

In our society, money plays a major part in our ability to govern ourselves, our families, our organizations, and our communities. Those who control money govern. Money is the universal measure that keeps track of our promises to one another (Block 1993).

Communities can't make and keep promises to citizens if they do not control the money. In our communities, our being publicly accountable for promises to families, their physical and mental well-being, education, and strength, reflects stewardship of precious financial and social resources.

This stewardship requires a full disclosure of how money is obtained and spent and the returns on those investments. The people who work in our educational, health care, and human service institutions must be more directly involved with the budgeting process. They should understand how financial decisions are made in their organizations and communities because financial decisions affect them, their work, and their own families.

If this devolution of responsibility is to be meaningful, it must be accompanied by the authority to manage and spend resources. Spending authority is a true measure of power and enhances a sense of ownership of the return on investment. The move to managed care, block grants, charter schools, and cash vouchers to individuals indicates a redistribution of power. This approach diverges from traditional, fragmented categorical funding which has historically been controlled by federal and state bureaucracies with limited input and flexibility at the local level.

Iowa's Decategorization Initiative, begun in the late 1980s, signaled the return of control over finances for social services to the community. The program is currently used in those counties that incorporate a majority of the state's population and it will be extended statewide in time. With participation from local leadership, both public and private, the counties establish Decategorization Boards. A planning process results in a vision for families and children and enables local boards to create a system of care that strengthens families while ensuring the safety of children. Resources from various state and federal funds are pooled at the local level, with the state serving as a central banker.

Funds from juvenile justice, education, child welfare and other local sources can be used creatively to reduce the number of children in out-of-home care. Savings achieved by developing new strategies for care can be reinvested in preventive measures. As a result of this creative approach to local control of finances, Iowa is creating a responsive community-based system of care.

RESULTS-ORIENTED CULTURE

The state of Oregon is the pioneer in results-based government. In the early 1980s, the governor, Neil Goldschmidt, launched an effort called Oregon Shines to create a long-term economic strategy for the state. The initiative evolved into what is known as Oregon Benchmarks. Over time the state has narrowed down several hundred outcomes into thirty-five core benchmarks and between fifteen and twenty urgent benchmarks. For example, in 1994 increased high school graduation rates became one of the core benchmarks. The goal is to increase high school graduation rates from 72 percent in 1990 to 93 percent in 2000 and 95 percent in 2010.

More and more state and local governments across the nation are becoming results oriented. They are also recognizing that narrow categorical approaches seldom succeed. They understand that progress linked to one set of results (e.g., decreased fetal alcohol syndrome among children) is linked to others (e.g., readiness to learn and performance in school). As communities better appreciate the interlocking nature of results and the fact that many programs involve the same families, they are creating long-term, collaborative agendas that both citizens and local service groups can understand and support. This change represents a dramatic departure from the traditional focus on categorical services and entitlements.

Social interventions are measured by their results for communities and families. Their welfare involves very real pain and suffering, hopes, and aspirations. The very nature of our work makes the shift from a service and entitlement culture to a results-oriented culture urgent. A results-oriented culture emphasizes holistic approaches to change, system ownership, and responsibility. Most of the valued social outcomes—resilient families, success in school, transition from welfare to work, and quality child care—result from clusters of social interventions. They are not the product or sole responsibility of any one program, but the result of a people acting together for a common purpose.

Communities must track various benchmarks of well-being over time. Progress on these benchmarks is kept before the public to exert an important critical tension among elected officials and program administrators to impel them to keep improving results. Communities, organizations, and citizens are motivated by their pride in supporting and facilitating positive results for people.

Transforming the Management of Social Programs

Efforts are underway at the federal, state, and local levels to transform traditional approaches to managing social programs. We are shifting away from a distant, isolated and centralized government to an increasingly democratic partnership between the government and its citizens—a family-friendly government. It is a collaboration and partnership marked by public stewardship and enhanced self-governance. It is a partnership characterized by an expanding circle of caring relationships, an accountability for real results for children and families, and family and community ownership of both the relationships and the results.

In Figure 2, the characteristics of both the traditional perspective on governance and decision making and the emerging perspective on self-governance are presented.

It is clear that new systems of social governance and management in the public sector are needed. Local problems call for local solutions and leadership models that facilitate the capacity of communities and families to solve their own problems. We all, from the citizen receiving services to line workers, supervisors, managers, elected officials, and the community at large, must think about the big picture and our own responsibility for contributing to the success of the whole. The complexity of problems in the modern era calls on everyone to take responsibility for the processes and services that affect citizens.

FIGURE 2: **Transforming Social Governance
and Management of the Public Sector**

WHAT IS BEING TRANSFORMED	A LOOK INTO THE FUTURE
Distant Government and Bureaucracy	Self-governing Communities and Families
Centralized Leadership	Decentralized Power
Bureaucracy	Responsible Citizens
Top-Down Planning and Control	Broad-Based Decision Making
A Focus on the Trees—Not the Forest	Thinking in Terms of Community
Picket-Fence Programs	Coordinated, Multifaceted Programs
Fixed Structures	Flexible Relationships
Central Control of Information Systems	Open and Quality Information Systems
Little Concern for Results	Results-Oriented Culture

The nature of work in the service professions—health, education, and the human services—must move from an orientation of control and compliance to a model of emergent and adaptive growth. Individuals who possess a clear sense of organizational purpose must be willing to work across professional, organizational, and community boundaries. In Ossie Davis's words, people must look up from what they are doing and work as a team to bring about effective change. When people do look up from their separate tasks, they must be prepared to change their conception of how things should work. Everyone must be prepared to discover and rediscover what works best under continuously changing conditions. Everyone must be willing to embrace a results-oriented culture that provides families and children with what they want and need.

Transforming traditional public approaches to the management of social programs creates opportunities for partnership and collaboration between government and the community. Social programs by themselves are insufficient to overcome our social problems. Collaborative partnerships among the larger community, private institutions, individual citizens, and public programs hold the promise of a better future for our families and children.

CHAPTER 3

Community Partnerships through Self-Reflection and Dialogue

COMMUNITY VOICES The file must have been several inches thick. Each person at the table had a copy. The police chief opened his first. The young man's name was Jason. Everyone opened the files and began to read. Jason was in elementary school when agency workers first met him. At that time he was well behaved and an excellent student. The focus then was on an older brother, who was running away from home. No attention was paid to Jason. Over the years, Jason's life fell apart. He was arrested at the age of 16. He was now in prison.

At the table were the district's assistant U.S. attorney, the superintendent of public instruction, the directors of the department of social services, juvenile services, and mental health, the county attorney, and the county manager. They had gathered that evening to begin what would become both a personal and community journey and an ongoing dialogue. Their goal was to reflect as individuals and as a community on what had gone wrong and to design community partnerships that would support and strengthen families and children.

What became apparent as they read the file was that Jason's story and that of his family had been known to each of their separate systems and the community. But over the course of the years, from the time he was six years of age, both Jason and his family had fallen through the cracks. The system, community, and family had not worked together. Information was not shared. Red flags were missed. Opportunities were lost.

As each person finished reading, he or she closed the file. It was quiet. Time was suspended. Each individual reflected on what he or she had just read. Questions circled through the heads of everyone present. What could "I," what could "we," have done differently to prevent this tragedy? How can "I," how can "we," begin to work together to break this vicious cycle where we seem unable to learn from our mistakes? What will it take to enable us to close ranks and come together as a community?

A Window of Opportunity

The process of social transformation has a cyclic, almost seasonal quality to it. But it builds up and plays itself out over decades and generations rather than over months. Societies in transition experience severe social disruptions that, when they happen, seem sudden. In fact, they have been building for a long time. Fortunately, as spring follows winter, disrupted societies possess an innate capacity to self-organize and remake themselves. With the first warm rays of spring, society begins to experiment with new social structures. Society begins to uncover and reflect on its values. New values, beliefs, and behaviors begin to emerge. But, just as social chaos did not spring up overnight, reasserting social order and reshaping our culture will take years. Social order is reasserted through a process of collective and individual reflection, dialogue, and new partnerships between community and families.

W\e are in the spring of a cycle of profound social transformation

We are in the spring of such a cycle. Our industrial society is being transformed and replaced by an information society. Large-scale economic and technological changes have disrupted community and family relationships. As these changes have taken hold, traditional patterns and rules for social order have weakened. In many of our neighborhoods and homes, these relationships and rules for behavior have slipped away.

We are beginning to see the tips of an emergent self-governing culture and new social institutions— more flexible funding relationships, more open management models, greater access to information and collaboration. In all of this we are experiencing a dramatic devolution and realignment of power and authority. We have reason to be optimistic. Societies built around increasingly open social structures, accessible information, and partnership will produce greater freedom and order. The social structures and relationships we create now will shape and design our lives for years to come.

We have reason to be optimistic— openness will produce greater freedom and order.

The transformation will not be painless. It will require a good deal of self-reflection. It will require a lot of dialogue. It will require all of "us," in the words of the vice president, Al Gore, following the tragedy in Littleton, Colorado, "to change" if we are to honor those children who died. The temptation will always be present to return to paternalistic and bureaucratic ways of doing things. The temptation will always be present to give our power away and blame others for our circumstances. The temptation will always be present to fall back on values that separate and isolate us. But the transformation will occur. It will take place one individual, one family, one organization, and one community at a time.

REFLECTIONS IN THE LOOKING GLASS

When Alice peered through the looking glass, she tried to make out what was on the other side. She peered as through a misty veil into a looking-glass house. She tried to make out the detail in the rooms. She tried to imagine the lives, motivations, and values of the people who lived in the house. In fact, what Alice saw was in part a reflection of her imagination. What she saw was in part a reflection of herself.

When those gathered around the community table looked into Jason's file, they were trying to piece together the details that would explain what happened. The veil was no less transparent. The picture was no less fuzzy. What they did make out in Jason's looking-glass house were the fragmented personal and family efforts at change. What they saw were missed opportunities, broken promises, poor communication, and a string of poor outcomes. What they saw in Jason's looking-glass community were similar, fragmented community efforts. What they saw in Jason's story was in large measure a reflection of themselves and what exists within their own systems.

Achieving an orderly and safe society is not just about chang-ing Jason's view of the world—were it so simple. A transformation on the order that is necessary requires that we all must change because all these things are linked. Chief Seattle recognized this when he observed that, "All things are connected like the blood which unites one family. Man did not weave the web of life; he is merely one strand in it. Whatever he does to the web he does to himself." We might add that what we see in the web, we can see in ourselves if we look.

To transform ourselves we must look into the looking glass through a new lens. We must look into our own looking-glass houses as well as those who need support. We must be prepared to reflect on how we must change ourselves if we are to engage others in the pro-cess of change. In reflecting on how to bring order and stability to our communities and families, we find direction in three guideposts: a clear sense of purpose, a willingness to make the change we want to see in ourselves, and an understanding that the path to collective order begins with personal self-control and self-governance.

COMMON PURPOSE AND THE TRAGEDY OF THE COMMONS

In 1968, Garrett Hardin wrote about a concept he called "the tragedy of the commons," a concept that still has relevance today. He observed that, when individuals, families, or organizations take responsibility for only their narrow interest or "part," they unwittingly contribute to the plundering of the commons—the community, their families, and social institutions. Elinor Ostrom (1993) illustrated this concept with the analogy of the overfishing of the Georges Bank off the coast of New England. Lacking good information about the pool of fish available or good commu-nications among the fishermen about how many fish were being taken each season from the limited pool, each individual fisher-man was left to maximize his narrow self-interest by taking as many fish as he could from the ocean. The fish population collapsed from the ungoverned fishing. Economic ruin descended on once-thriving communities.

A parallel can be found in the contemporary breakdown of community and family life. Social institutions when governed by narrow self-interest and not by common purpose act to maximize that interest. Each social institution seeks to maximize the amount of resources it extracts from the community. Juvenile justice, education, public welfare, and mental health programs grow larger and larger. Lacking common purpose and good communication and often competitively at war with one another, they ultimately exhaust the public's good will.

When the heads of various systems sat down to ponder what had happened to Jason, they discovered that they had all been working separately with Jason and his family over the years—and they did not know it! They discovered that they did not know one another personally or professionally. They were even more unaware of the efforts of family, friends and neighbors, clergy, or employers to support Jason and his family. Working in a "cloud of ignorance," they had been treating their failures or successes as separately won or lost. In fact, their failures and successes were intimately intertwined. They had failed to see Jason in the context of either his family or his community. They had seen isolation and social problems when they needed to look for connections and strengths. They had been competing and battling over organizational turf and political self-interest when they needed to look to cooperation and common purpose.

We often treat our successes and failures as separately won or lost—in fact they are intimately intertwined with the success and failures of our families and communities.

BE THE CHANGE

Gandhi observed that the most effective way to bring about change in others is to model that change in oneself. If Gandhi were at the table with the community leaders or the dinner table of families around the country, he would call on those present "to be the change they want to see in others."

The values and behaviors that we attribute to healthy communities and families—trust, dialogue, interdependence, cooperation, and purpose—are often in direct conflict with the values and practices of bureaucratic systems and narrow self-interested individuals. Superintendents of public instruction, directors of public welfare agencies, and heads of juvenile justice programs often see education, public social services, and the prevention of crime and violence as their responsibility. They are reluctant to engage the community in a partnership for change. In turn, many citizens and parents see education, public welfare, and the prevention of crime and violence as responsibilities of the system. They are reluctant to join the system in a partnership for change.

This inability to see outside oneself is called parallel process in psychology. It is also called a vicious circle. Systems own community institutions, their interventions, and the clients they serve. Citizens turn over ownership and responsibility for institutions, interventions, and families to systems. In Chicago, Mayor Daly took over the public school system in 1997. In some low-performing schools, all the personnel, principals, teachers, and instructional aides, were dismissed. The scarlet letter of failure was attached to the school. When school success is not achieved, everyone blames the principals and teachers. No one dismisses the community or its parents. Accountability is not shared. To be the change that we want to see in others, both systems and communities must model shared responsibility and accountability for outcomes. We know systems and citizens cannot achieve complex outcomes until they work together collaboratively. We know that a part is not responsible for the whole. Both must be willing to change.

SELF-CONTROL AND SELF-GOVERNANCE

It is frequently argued that people naturally resist change, and that is why we have command-and-control systems. In top-down social institutions where the top thinks and the bottom acts, people are told what to do by people who ostensibly know better. A shift in perspectives holds that people do not, in fact, dislike change. What they dislike is *being changed*. They dislike being left out of the creative process and then told to take responsibility for something they had no part in creating.

Self-organization, change, and creativity come naturally to people—just look at the face of a child. The spark in a child's eye reflects a world of possibility and creativity. Children are willing to draw outside the lines. People, not just children, are committed to things they help create. They draw meaning and self-definition from what they create. They do not lend their full energy, talent, and time to those things for which they feel no creative ownership. In psychology, this phenomenon is called locus of control. People like to have a sense of being in control of their lives. Control and self-governance, initiating and making one's own decisions and commitments, are essential components of personal and community self-esteem.

By nature, most of us react poorly to efforts by others to control us. We resist such efforts either actively or passively. Control-and-compliance does not engage people's spirit or commitment—just look at the faces of many working adults. Control-and-compliance dulls the spark in the eye and the impulse toward creativity. Many families resist turning to public welfare because of the price they are asked to pay in control and self-esteem. Many individuals do not seek mental health services for depression because to do so is to be labeled as different, not normal, and not self-sufficient. Many students do not fully commit themselves to traditional public education because the price of admission is compliance and passivity. Yet most of us will seek help and are open to change when we are met with respect, partnership, and shared accountability.

Dialogue

How do we end this vicious cycle of poor outcomes for communities and families? Ostrom (1993) observed that some organizations and communities are able to break the shackles of such cycles by focusing on factors *internal* to a given group, family, organization, or community. Successful groups and individuals resist the temptation to externalize the blame for their problems. They resist the temptation to give away their power for solving problems.

There are three factors that help break the cycle of poor outcomes: developing better ways to communicate with one another, building trust, and fostering a shared sense of future. All are within our reach.

Dialogue is the medium by which we effectively communicate with one another and shape a shared future through community and family partnerships. We talk. We listen. We connect. If you remember, the word *dialogue* has two complementary translations, the more recent definition being "through (*dia*) words (*logos*)." To communicate—to understand one another—we must inquire into the assumptions and meaning behind our words. An earlier translation of the word *logos* is "relationship." Dialogue involves developing a sense of understanding and relationship with one another. It is the way we connect all the parts—the people that make up the whole—the community and family.

Dialogue involves changing the way we communicate, see, and connect one to another. It provides a tool for exposing the underlying values and mental models that lock us into unproductive cycles. It provides us with a tool for capturing diverse perspectives and forging new and more productive relationships. Dialogue is used to create what Ellinor and Gerard (1998) call practice fields for building a common foundation of understanding, trust, improved relationships, and a sense of a shared future. The self-governance approach and tools outlined in the second part of this book describe the creation and operation of such practice fields in the community. If we are to work effectively together to achieve common purposes, we, like a team or an orchestra, must practice.

COMMUNICATING WITH ONE ANOTHER

Effective communication involves understanding people from diverse backgrounds and divergent perspectives. The fuel that drives new partnerships is found in bringing together such people. Dialogue helps us do just that. Tapping into the creative energy associated with inclusive participatory dialogues is a challenge. We typically regard diversity and differences of opinion as threats to our own worldview. Partnerships can emerge when we reframe diversity and differences as opportunities for learning, growth, and cooperation. Dialogue helps us do this by defusing our tendency to jump to conclusions and short circuit our learning. For the physicist David Bohm (1995), dialogue occurs when people understand what is on the minds of others without coming to any conclusions or making any judgments. Both actions are essential for creating new understandings and shared meaning.

Effective dialogue is a reflective process where we move our chair back and listen for shared meaning.

Suspending judgment calls for each of us to get outside of his or her own box and listen. Judging is a process by which we divide reality into parts and differences of opinion into competing interests. Judging is a competitive, exclusionary process in which there is only one right answer. It reflects either/or thinking. Suspending judgment opens the door to learning and partnership. Suspending judgment and creating partnerships requires both/and thinking. Your way and my way together perhaps yield a third way. One plus one can equal three. Dialogue asks us to recapture what may be a long-gone childhood curiosity to explore the meaning and purpose behind the words and create new meanings and purposes. It helps us to accept that there are a number of different paths to the same results.

Effective dialogue is a reflective process. In it we move from being on automatic pilot to using words, inference, and action to question the beliefs and assumptions behind the words and actions of others. It is what Argyris (1992) called double-loop learning. It involves our turning off the automatic pilot, moving the chair back, and listening for shared meaning. If we are to move to a different future, the first hurdle we must clear is ourselves.

BUILDING TRUST

Suspending judgment and identifying and exploring the assumptions behind our words and behaviors contribute to the development of trust between individuals. Building trust between citizens and government, line workers and their managers, parents and children, neighbor and neighbor is perhaps our greatest challenge. Without trust, almost everything else is impossible. With it, everything is possible. Building trust involves creating a space for dialogue, a practice field where people feel safe and respected. Creating a safe forum for communication means that individuals can acknowledge and learn from their vulnerability. It means that they can learn from not knowing everything. It means that, without being punished, they can identify what is not working as well as it should. It involves being able to identify, share, and learn from our mistakes.

Building trust involves creating public spaces and forums for dialogues where people feel safe and respected.

Trust is an expression of both vulnerability and openness. An expression of vulnerability creates space for others to come forward with their contributions. An expression of openness creates an opportunity for others to participate in the creative process. Together, they ask that everyone's talent be contributed to community building and family strengthening.

CREATING THE SENSE OF A SHARED FUTURE

In the aftermath of the tragedy at Littleton, Colorado, an individual remarked in an interview on CNN that he did not think that such a tragedy could happen in that kind of community. The implication is that problems happen to people who are not like us. Until nations, communities, or families feel that they are at risk and vulnerable, they will not be moved to the kind of introspection and dialogue that is essential for meaningful change to occur. Individuals in positions of power who benefit from the status quo may also block efforts by the less powerful to alter the rules of the game even when there is a widespread call for change. Those who are less powerful may need some external assistance and support. The less powerful will also need to turn to an internal moral compass—higher voice—to support changes that threaten their personal security.

Creating a sense of the shared future begins with a candid dialogue about the state of the community, its social institutions, and the family. A sense of shared future is fostered when the conversation shifts from assumptions and judgments about the approaches and motivations of others to a clear focus on the outcomes that we desire in common, irrespective of political persuasion or interest group. For example, in the spring of 1999, the city of Seattle, Washington, proposed to issue charters within the public school system. There the conversation had moved beyond either/or to encompass both/and, beyond defending the status quo to articulate a concern and focus on school success for all. The result exemplifies the benefits of identifying an acceptable common ground that combines the flexibility and freedom of charter schools with the public school concerns for equal opportunity and universal education.

Community and Family Partnerships

Community partnerships acknowledge the multilayered complexity associated with efforts to strengthen families. Such partnerships recognize the nature of decision making and self-governance as a nested process in which leadership and responsibility are shared in overlapping concentric circles. For partnerships to be effective, they must be participatory and democratic. Everyone must share power, decision making, and accountability. Strong communities and families are nothing more and nothing less than webs of relationships and commitments one to another. Such partnerships rest on a three-legged stool of respect, ownership, and public accountability. Partnerships are strengthened when partners respect one another's contributions. Ownership is broadly distributed. Accountability is public.

RESPECT

Self-governing communities and families recognize and celebrate diversity. Diversity of perspective, talent, culture, and contribution is the lifeblood of successful self-organization and adaptation. Diversity is recognized when participants are able to contribute that difference, a talent, or perspective. Respect for diversity is the first leg on the three-legged stool of successful partnerships. Ellinor and Gerard (1998) observed that respect lies at the heart of our ability to value diversity. An intrinsic characteristic of individuals is their desire to be recognized for making a difference. Such recognition is another way of saying I exist, I am worthwhile, I have made a difference.

Respect lies at the heart of our ability to value diversity in our communities

Stewardship in self-governing communities and families is about seeing to it that unique talents are recognized and contributed. An example can be found in our schools.

Public schools in recent years have become larger and larger. Their very size increases the likelihood that individual students are overlooked or lost in the crowd. Isolated individuals—loners—are more at risk of school failure. Creating smaller schools or breaking large schools up into smaller "homes" within the same school increases the chance that each student's talent and contribution whether in the arts, sports, or academics will be recognized.

SHARED OWNERSHIP AND RESPONSIBILITY

People have a greater sense of responsibility for what they own. Homeowners take better care of their property than do renters. Students who take part in their school feel a greater sense of pride and personal motivation to do well in school. Parents involved in developing plans for strengthening their children feel more ownership for those plans and are more likely to follow through on their responsibilities. Shared ownership and responsibility is the second leg of effective partnerships.

Dialogue helps people identify where they can make a contribution to the group. Open communication helps others recognize the individual or the group's part and contribution to the whole. To be a partner is to share in creating the future. Ownership, communication, and a sense of interdependence are integral to effective partnerships.

Maureen Joy is a predominantly African American charter school in Durham, North Carolina. When you listen to its teachers, staff, parents, and students, you hear something quite extraordinary. They all sound as if they own the place. They are, in fact, co-owners in an exciting education experiment. Through extensive dialogue and participation and a commitment to accountability and school success for everyone, they are in pursuit of a dream. In recent years, they have achieved nearly universal parent participation in shaping that dream. The dream of school success for all is possible when a community is committed to its school and a school is committed to give back to its community.

PUBLIC ACCOUNTABILITY

Open communication and clear accountability for one's contribution serves to put people on their best behavior. The gap between values and behavior grows when planning happens behind closed doors and involves only the usual suspects. When roles and contributions are clear to the public, whomever the relevant public is, open information places a natural group pressure on all parties to step up and perform at their best. Open communication and public accountability act like sunlight. They cleanse communities and families of unproductive and secretive behaviors. They provide the light and energy that nourishes and brings out the best in people.

In Forsyth County, North Carolina, the community's leaders in education and the human services have committed themselves to both collaboration and public accountability. To facilitate both ends, the community has begun to put in place The Jason Network, an information system that links all the key players in the community together to share information and accountability for results. The goal is learn from one another and to ensure that no future Jasons fall through the cracks.

COMMUNITIES AND FAMILIES IN PARTNERSHIP

Through a process of self-reflection, we come to realize what the cartoon figure Pogo meant when he said that we have met the enemy and it is us. The present level of distrust and disdain for public institutions and government is an ominous sign for a democracy. In a democratic society, the public schools, public welfare, mental health, and juvenile justice programs are the institutional tools for performing the public's will. They—our public institutions—are, as Magaziner (1995) observed, us. To be at war with them is to be at war with ourselves.

Somewhere along the line as our government and social institutions grew larger and more powerful, they became disconnected from us, the public. In part, this disconnection may be a result of our optimism with government and social engineers. We were led to believe and we wanted to believe that larger and more powerful social institutions could by themselves fix our social problems and raise our children. They cannot. Lacking the public's involvement and ownership for its own institutions, those institutions are destined to fail. Lacking the public's involvement in its own children and the institutions that serve them, those institutions lose sight of the bottom line: results for families and children. Lacking the public's involvement and commitment to be part of the solution, we are unable to attend to the small personal details, responsibilities, and follow-through that are the essence of everyday life. When small things are left undone, the long-term consequences are overwhelming.

Government can help put the public back into its public institutions through the continued devolution of power and decision making. It can do so by creating space and social structures that foster dialogue and meaningful public participation in the design, redesign, and continuous evaluation of its social institutions. It reestablishes trust through expanded community and family partnerships.

The Vietnam War Memorial in Washington, D.C., serves as appropriate metaphor for reclaiming our social institutions. The memorial is a "public memorial," designed in a way that invites, in fact demands, the public to participate to find meaning. Only through direct participation can individuals discover fully the personal and collective significance of that war. A long, black marble wall, the memorial is largely hidden by a rise in a grassy knoll. It is not until you are almost upon it that it rises up to greet you. It stretches out like a black serpent in front of you. You are drawn near to make out the print that covers its face. The lettering across the memorial names every American who died in the war. You must come face to face with the memorial to search out, find, and touch the name of a lost family member or friend. To participate is to make it personal. Up and down the line, individuals are making rubbings. A piece of paper is placed over a name. A pencil is rubbed over the paper to draw the name out. The family member or friend then has a remembrance to take back home. The memorial makes a direct connection with its visitors and in the process, they are deeply moved.

Social institutions that personally engage citizens in decision making and day-to-day operations are sowing the seeds of revitalization and democratic accountability. The city of Jacksonville, Florida, has established a Neighborhoods Services Division that is committed to help citizens build better neighborhoods through enhanced communication and partnership. It supports shared accountability for problem solving and celebrates its successful collaborations. It invites citizens to share in community building through an Annual Neighborhood Summit. Representatives from hundreds of neighborhood associations gather to share community-building ideas. They create and celebrate community together.

Self-governing communities and social institutions invite families and citizens to participate, define, and breathe life and purpose into them. The gap between the public and its social institutions is bridged through self-reflection, dialogue, and partnerships to strengthen communities and families. We are unified and enlivened by our diversity and freedom.

Community Dialogues—
The Path to Self-Governance

To end the cycle of poor outcomes for communities and families, social institutions should be willing to change themselves and enter into broad, accountable partnerships with their publics and to engage in a process of open and continuous dialogue with those publics. Self-governance dialogues provide the path to heightened community and family self-governance and partnership. They build consensus around common purpose. They enhance communication and build trust. They share learning and accountability. They bring to the surface new approaches to strengthening community and family. They are a catalyst for thinking differently about what needs to be done and everyone's role in getting it done. By themselves, they are but an opportunity for change. But, when matched by a willingness on the part of institutions to open up and experiment, they hold the promise of significant change. And, when paired with community leadership and a broad-based commitment to follow through on promises, they can turn dreams into reality.

CHAPTER 4

Designing Self-Governance Dialogues

COMMUNITY VOICES   The headlines created a sensation in Raleigh, North Carolina. The grades were in. Poe Elementary, a school in Wake County, had been identified as "low performing." It had failed the ABCs of public education and performance in North Carolina. As a consequence, the school's principal was to be dismissed, and teachers would not be eligible for incentive awards. The school would be labeled a low-performing school for two years. It had been marked with the scarlet letter.

North Carolina's ABCs Accountability Model for grades K–8 established growth standards for every elementary and middle school in the state in 1996. Schools that received the right marks were eligible for incentive awards or other recognition. Outcomes were based on data collected during the 1996–1997 school year. The report cards for the 1,631 participating elementary and middle schools were the first of their kind in North Carolina.

Parents and teachers from Poe Elementary rose up in arms. The local newspaper, *The News and Observer,* ran lead stories for several days. The editorial pages bristled with objections to what many saw as a simplistic grading of school performance through standardized tests and the public humiliation of schools, their administrators, teachers, and students. Principals and administrators from the surrounding schools came to the principal's defense. The school district refused to comply with the requested dismissal of the principal. The North Carolina Department of Public Instruction backed down from the dismissal of the school principal, but the designation as a low-performing school and the penalties stood.

Paths to Self-Governance Dialogues

Many paths can lead to community dialogue, dialogues that themselves take their own twists and turns. In the case of Poe Elementary in Raleigh, North Carolina, dialogue was triggered when parents, students, and the educational community rallied in support of their principal and school. In Taos, New Mexico, it came from a growing concern among parents, schools, and the juvenile justice system about the rise in teen violence. Whatever the particular path, these dialogues share something in common. They all began with a single voice or the voice of a small group of people reacting to an unacceptable situation. Often, these groups are driven to fight back against an assault on order, dignity, and self-respect.

> Dialogue begins with a single voice responding to a situation it finds unacceptable.

In traveling the nation's backroads as the people's correspondent, Charles Kuralt discovered something important. He discovered that in every neighborhood, community, and state there exists *a conspiracy of good people.* They represent the potential association of men and women, who, although they may not even know one another, can be called to action on behalf of their community and its families. The poet Carl Sandburg referred to these people a *saving minority,* those always willing to be heard when they have to be heard.

> In every neighborhood, community and state there exists a "conspiracy of good people" to address that which needs to be addressed.
>
> CHARLES KURALT

This conspiracy of good people, this saving minority, reflects a personal moral voice that, when expressed through dialogue with others, can tap into the moral voice of the community. Those who first speak up are expressing a personal reaction to a discrepancy between how people are behaving and how they should behave. They see that blaming a principal for the failure of a school is both simplistic and a violation of their mutual responsibility. A community speaks up when there is a gap between what it observes and what it knows to be right. A self-governing community seeks to close that gap.

Designing Self-Governance Dialogues

This chapter provides an overview of how community self-governance dialogues can be used to catalyze and engage a community dissatisfied with the present state of affairs. The initial stage of setting up a community dialogue, including a brief discussion of self-governance and community learning, is described and the purposes, tasks, processes, and time frames associated with the dialogues are discussed.

A breakdown of the two-and-a-half day dialogue is provided. Subject, task, and sequence are deliberate. Principles for successfully engaging the community are highlighted. The chapter concludes with a review of common challenges to community self-governance dialogues and community self-governance. Chapters 5 through 7 provide a detailed outline of days one, two, and three.

SETTING THE STAGE

Setting the stage for a self-governance dialogue involves identifying a host, assessing common purpose and outcomes, and convening the community. Typically, stage-setting activity occurs between six weeks and two months before the actual dialogue. Six weeks or more are needed to ensure inclusive representation of the host institution and community in the dialogue.

DIALOGUE HOST

The host or sponsor for a community self-governance dialogue is often an agency or system that has the principal responsibility for achieving a common purpose and specific community outcomes. For example, schools may host dialogues on educational outcomes, child welfare agencies on adoption, foster care, and child abuse and neglect, and community welfare agencies on jobs for poor people or teen pregnancy. Many lead agencies or systems prefer to cohost community dialogues. For example, the welfare agency may cosponsor the dialogue on welfare reform with various employment-related agencies, advocacy groups, and the local chambers of commerce.

At other times, community self-governance dialogues are hosted by community collaboratives. Community collaboratives may be organized around broad areas of interest such as educational reform or they may focus on a more narrowly drawn topic such as teen pregnancy. For example, the United Way of Greenville, South Carolina, joined the Golden Strip Family Resource Center to host a community dialogue around welfare reform, literacy, and child abuse and neglect.

IDENTIFYING COMMON PURPOSE AND COMMUNITY OUTCOMES

The host agency or consortium has the responsibility of identifying the focus or common purpose of the self-governance dialogue. Common purpose refers to both the overall vision the community seeks to achieve and the specific outcomes or results that the community hopes to secure for itself and its families in support of that vision.

A small representative group of community stakeholders is convened initially to identify a common purpose, both as a vision and as specific outcomes. In Idaho, a loosely knit consortium of citizens and agencies was convened by the state's Children's Trust Fund and its Health and Welfare Agency to plan a community dialogue for later that spring. More than twenty individuals gathered to set the purpose and outcomes and plan the agenda for a self-governance dialogue. Their vision was one of strengthening communities and families. The specific results sought by the community included reductions in teen violence, child abuse, and neglect. The selection of a set of outcomes acknowledges their interdependent nature. Success in one area is coupled to success in other areas. The community representatives also sought to enhance the local leadership capacity for families and children.

CONVENING THE COMMUNITY

People in every community across the nation nod their heads in support of the statement that it takes a strong community and healthy families to raise children. They agree that families cannot successfully raise their children without the help of the community. Self-governance dialogues convene the community on behalf of families.

Host communities and organizations are advised to gather a broad cross-section of the community. In attendance should be representatives from the civic, religious, business, media, political, and nonprofit service communities, in addition to individuals from the host system or agency. Between 25 and 40 percent of those in attendance should be from the community at large, and, for a community self-governance dialogue on education reform, might include parents, students, and the civic, business, religious, media, political, and service communities. Between 60 and 75 percent should be drawn from the educational community itself, administrators, teachers, support staff, policy analysts, and others. Without a sufficient presence from those outside the system in question, the diverse voices and contributions of the community will be lost.

Framework for Dialogue and Community Learning

Self-governance dialogues reflect a philosophical framework of participative management and community empowerment. It is an optimistic philosophy that asserts that by engaging our communities, meaningful, real-time change can be achieved. A community fully engaged in its own governance can in turn change unproductive behaviors and beliefs. Order and well-being can be achieved even for our most disrupted families when a community's talent and capacity is fully engaged on its own behalf.

BEYOND THE USUAL SUSPECTS

The self-governance dialogue changes the traditional hierarchical and fragmented approach to a community learning process. It moves away from an overreliance on top-down expertise. A switch is made from linear, time-consuming approaches headed up by the usual suspects such as agency administrators, policy analysts, planners, and the like to an integrated, dynamic approach involving everyone's voice.

Rather than breaking change into a segmented process of planning, implementation, and evaluation, the self-governance dialogues collapse these elements into a single continuous process of adaptation and learning. All the participants engage in and are responsible for planning, implementing, and evaluating their contributions toward the community's vision and outcomes. Both the process and its facilitators tap the community's collective expertise in understanding the present and creating the future. Self-governance dialogues tap into a community's capacity to self-organize and generate context-specific solutions to the challenges it faces. Facilitators help set the stage and tone for the dialogue, then stand back.

A COMMUNITY CREATES ITS OWN FUTURE

Self-governance dialogues place the community and its families in the position of taking responsibility for creating their future. This responsibility is spurred on when representatives from the host agency, education, welfare, or the human services acknowledge that they cannot achieve the community vision or secure the desired outcomes on their own. The process is taken one step further when experts ask for assistance from the community. The combined contributions, resources, and capacity of the community are needed to be successful.

Facilitators through a process of inclusive dialogue tap the community's collective expertise in understanding its present and creating its future.

Acknowledging the limits of professional or system expertise opens the doors to new ways of thinking. It also acknowledges what the community already knows. The community knows that systems by themselves cannot improve education, end poverty, curb teen violence, or put our moral house back in order. By engaging the community in the process of inventing new approaches to valued outcomes, a broad base for public ownership and accountability is built. The public will own and care for what it has a hand in creating.

SHIFTING VALUES AND BEHAVIORAL MAPS

Self-governance dialogues are fundamentally about shifting values and behavioral maps. Such dialogues place the responsibility for change squarely on the shoulders of the involved players. They acknowledge that, in order to create a better future, we must overcome the present. We have to alter many of our own values and behaviors. Rather than externalizing the barriers to change, the focus is on what we alone have responsibility for and authority over—changing ourselves.

Self-governance dialogues offer communities the opportunity to take responsibility for their own future.

By focusing on better outcomes for communities and families, self-governance dialogues enable the system and the citizens it represents to be reflective and critical about past and present approaches to securing that future. Self-governance dialogues constantly affirm our sense of common purpose, values, and vision. They bring valued outcomes within reach by keeping us open to continuous change in our behaviors and approaches.

PRIVATE RESPONSIBILITY AND COMMUNITY ACCOUNTABILITY

Self-governance dialogues stress both private responsibility and community accountability for results. No one program or individual is responsible for or owns any particular problem or outcome. In a democracy the community and its citizens own its challenges and are responsible for achieving a common vision and purpose. Public and private agencies, institutions, and citizens serve the community by helping it achieve that vision and purpose.

Community ownership of both the problems and the promise of better results engenders a creative tension in all the players, inspiring them to do their part. When the promise of better outcomes is kept before the public and progress or lack of progress toward those results is tallied, the social intervention process is kept fresh and flexible. Through a process of collective experimentation and feedback, the community continuously revises those approaches that do not work and holds onto those that do.

Self-Governance Dialogues at a Glance

The term *self-governance dialogue* refers to a community event that transpires over a two-and-a-half day period. The dialogues are designed to accommodate groups ranging in size from a couple dozen to several hundred individuals and are facilitated by outside consultants.

Self-governance dialogues draw on many concepts, themes, and techniques from the field of community and organizational development. They also draw from the ideas of authors and practitioners of whole-system change, real-time strategic change, open-field technology, performance consulting, search and future-search

---

Self-Governance Dialogues At a Glance

Day 1:

MORNING
- Building community through dialogue
- Results and change through self-governance
- Establishing a common reality

AFTERNOON
- Moving forward by looking back—mapping the present
- Reporting the present

Day 2:

MORNING
- Shifting to the future—altering one's paradigm
- Creating the future—mapping what will be

AFTERNOON
- Continuing to map what will be
- Reporting the future
- Community promises for change

Day 3:

MORNING
- From community promises to action plans
- Commitment to public accountability

---

conferences, and self-evaluation. The process plays out across eight developmental stages, beginning with building community through dialogue and concluding with a community and organizational commitment to self-governance and public accountability. Each stage builds on and refers to the ones that proceed it, creating a process of constant emergent change and learning. The dialogues result in community action plans centered around achieving an overall vision and specific outcomes for families and children. The outline on the previous page highlights the process.

DAY 1: MORNING

Registration and refreshments begin at 8:30 a.m. The conference continues until 4:00 p.m., with an on-site lunch break of forty-five minutes. People sit in groups of between eight and ten individuals. The groupings reflect a mix of host organization staff (such as a school), community stakeholders (business, religious, civic, political, media, and related organizations and associations), and consumers (such as parents, children, and others). Each group is assigned an outcome (for example, high school graduation rate or teen pregnancy) to work on throughout the two-and-a-half day dialogue.

The first day opens with a series of exercises to build and strengthen a sense of community among the assembled participants and to provide a safe environment for the expression of divergent perspectives on achieving common purposes. The first exercise is an icebreaker referred to as the limits of expertise. The individuals within each group are asked to recount a story about an occasion on which they were thought to be the expert although they were not. This exercise introduces group members to one another and begins to level the playing field for participants by acknowledging the limits of everyone's expertise. Group members introduce themselves and recount their story to the entire group. Lessons from the story are shared and discussed.

After the icebreaker, the dialogue facilitators go over the agenda. Feedback and clarification are obtained on the community vision and the outcomes that will serve as the centerpieces for the dialogue. Outcomes may be clarified or added. The discussion outlines the framework for identifying and mapping the gap between present and future outcomes for families in the community and the gap between present and future strategies to secure future outcomes. The approach identifies the role of reflective self-evaluation and the self-governance process in the community. Facilitators set the stage for the dialogue.

The second task of the morning is the establishment of a common reality, a common jumping off point for dialogue participants. The process of establishing such a base of understanding involves collecting a mixture of quantitative data and personal stories related to the outcomes the community has selected for itself. Both the data and the stories are figuratively and literally placed in the center of the room. This information represents everything that the community knows about itself in relation to the identified outcomes and the families behind those outcomes. Communities, organizations, and families frequently base their inferences and actions around a particular issue on limited information. Until everyone has an opportunity to tell everything he or she knows about a challenge, the community is operating with incomplete knowledge. A common understanding is essential to the pursuit of common purposes and effective collective action.

DAY 1: AFTERNOON

In the afternoon, the groups create a "map" of how the present system works in relation to each outcome. Each group has a piece of butcher paper, between six and twelve feet in length, on which the present system is mapped.

The groups are also presented with a packet containing pieces of paper with pictures of plumbing pipe. When placed on the butcher paper, the pipe pieces will represent the various twists and turns that the present system takes in yielding a result, an outcome such as a reduction in the welfare rolls. The pieces of pipe come in different lengths that can be used to represent not only the decisions and contributions of various community players but also the length of time taken to produce those decisions and contributions.

When finished, each group reports on its graphic representation of the current system, what works and what does not. The groups identify where the process flows and where it becomes stuck. Individuals find this exercise illuminating; they also find it fun. Everyone plays a part in creating the map of the present. Most are familiar with their own parts, but many are frequently unaware of the contributions and difficulties experienced by others in the community and even fellow employees in their own organizations. They are surprised and delighted with their emergent collective understanding of how the current system works, its strengths and weaknesses.

DAY 2: MORNING

The morning of day two begins with a discussion about how we shift paradigms, our ways of thinking and perceiving. Participants are asked to think about why it is that we often know better than we do. Participants are asked to identify those beliefs and values that hold current practices in place even when we know that we could do better. Dissatisfaction with present outcomes for families and children provides us with a certain level of motivation to think outside the box. Participants and voices new to our systems, voices from business, the religious community, and civic and political associations, offer communities an opportunity to entertain fresh perspectives on how our business might be conducted differently.

A combination of stories and videotapes is used to illustrate processes for shifting the way we think about something, the way we solve problems. For example, a clip from the movie *Apollo 13* is used to illustrate problem-solving skills in a crisis. With only limited oxygen left on board Apollo 13, the members of the ground crew abandon their specific roles and functions and follow a collective problem-solving process. The rule book is thrown out. The focus shifts from what the original system was designed to do to what it actually can do now.

The central task of the second morning involves beginning to map the future. Using a new length of butcher paper and set of pipe pieces, each group maps a new and more effective way of doing business in the community. In mapping the future participants are asked to begin at the end; that is, they begin with the outcome and map backward. The challenge is to engage the capacity and resources of a diverse community to arrive by more effective path(s) to identified community outcomes. The challenge is not to think of the community as a surrogate for a professional service system. Group participants free themselves of the present and think differently about improving outcomes by using the contributions of the various players at the table and in the community.

DAY 2: AFTERNOON

The afternoon finds participants continuing to work on their map of the future. By thinking about what works in the current system and redesigning what does not work, they craft an improved approach. By thinking about the potential contributions of community participants who have not formally been a part of the system, they devise new and creative partnerships involving both the formal and informal system, professionals and ordinary citizens alike.

The afternoon concludes with groups presenting their maps of the future to the assembled participants. Questions are asked and new ideas, approaches, and assumptions explained. The maps provide a pictorial and conceptual starting point for community action, for building community consensus for actions that will need the support of many of those who have assembled for the dialogue.

On the basis of these maps and the individual and collective learning that has occurred, each person is asked in the afternoon to make a written and signed promise to act on behalf of the community, a "community promise for performance." Each participant is asked to identify a change in his or her own behavior that will contribute to securing an identified community outcome. Participants are also directed to request a change from an individual or some other program in the name of improving a community outcome. The community promises provide an additional input to the creation of action plans on behalf of the community's vision and outcomes.

DAY 3: MORNING

On the morning of the third and last day of the dialogue, groups begin to develop action plans. Continuing to work in their original groups, participants brainstorm a list of actions to be taken in support of the identified outcome at their table. Armed with the list, they are then asked to prioritize the three most important actions. When they have completed this list, they report their recommendations to the entire group. The actions linked to the identified outcomes are recorded on flip-chart paper and placed on the wall for the entire group to observe. After reviewing and recording all the action plans linked to the specific outcomes, the entire group identifies strategies and actions that cut across the various outcomes and compiles them as part of an overall action plan.

The work of the day concludes with a discussion of next steps. This phase of the dialogue includes a voluntary sign-up for a community performance team that will be responsible for tracking and reporting progress on the dialogue actions and outcomes. The role of the performance team and its relationship to collaborative self-governance structures in the community is made clear to all. Community members who sign up for the team reflect the community's commitment to follow up. The community self-governance dialogue ends between 12:00 and 1:00 p.m. on the third day.

Rules of Engagement with the Community

Over the past couple of years, several important lessons have been learned about conducting self-governance dialogues. These lessons are referred to here as rules of engagement with the community. They represent those rules or principles that are nonnegotiable if community self-governance dialogues are to succeed.

RULES OF ENGAGEMENT WITH THE COMMUNITY

The whole community must be in the room.

The group must put purpose and outcomes over problems.

There must be no blame, no shame, and no enemies.

Self-managed learning is encouraged.

Values and beliefs that impede change must be uncovered.

Separately a part; together the whole.

THE WHOLE COMMUNITY MUST BE IN THE ROOM

Irrespective of the outcome that a community decides to pursue, the whole community must be in the room if the dialogue is to be successful. Diverse perceptions of the challenges the community faces are needed to obtain an understanding of the whole. New partnerships within the community are needed to secure those outcomes and that vision. Everyone's talent, authority, perspective, and skill are needed to meet the challenges facing our communities and families. If the community is racially diverse, those who come to the table must be racially diverse. If the community has a high proportion of older adults, a high portion of those at the table must be older. When you look out across the room at a community dialogue you must be able to see a representative cross-section of your community if your dialogue is to be successful.

In self-governance dialogues, the invitation list might vary slightly depending on the vision and outcomes a community is pursuing. Although the numbers may vary among the different categories of invitees, the categories themselves hold fairly uniform across communities. For a dialogue held in Alamance County, North Carolina, the host organization was the county child welfare agency. The vision for the dialogue was family permanence. The outcome focus included reductions in child abuse and neglect, the number of children in foster care, and improvements in health care access. The invitation list included the following (the numbers in parentheses indicating the number of people invited from that sector):

Host county child welfare agency (12)	Media (2)
Community volunteers (6)	Courts (4)
Faith community (6)	Public health (2)
Business community (4)	Schools (6)
Elected officials (3)	Police (4)
Families (10)	Civic associations (6)
Nonprofit agencies (12)	Neighborhood associations (8)

We have found that it is easier to get "the professional system" into the room; it is a challenge to get the whole community there because it is harder to engage the informal community, business and religious communities, families, media, elected officials, and civic associations. What makes the difference is the use of personal networks. If event organizers employ their personal networks, who they know, they can obtain a good cross-section of the community.

In conducting community dialogues across the country, we have developed what we call the rule of thirty-five. If a community sends out written invitations to a list of seventy-five, one hundred and fifty, or two hundred individuals, thirty-five will show up for the dialogue. If organizers employ personal networks when choosing whom to invite, they will get close to the number they go after. An optimal number for a community dialogue has been between fifty-five and eighty individuals. The size of the group depends in part on the number of outcomes that are the focus of the dialogue and the time available for group reports. Groups of thirty-five can be just as effective as groups of eighty or more. In Alamance County, seventy-eight individuals participated in the community dialogue. In Athens, Georgia, nearly two hundred individuals participated in a self-governance dialogue.

THE GROUP MUST PUT PURPOSE AND OUTCOMES ABOVE PROBLEMS

We have found that communities and organizations are motivated by purpose, the recognition of success within the community, and an opportunity to create even higher levels of success. In developing a common database around the community's vision, outcomes, and families, we stay away from traditional need- and problem-oriented data. Characterizing families and children by their problems and deficits is disempowering and paternalistic. Problems and deficits do not motivate families and communities to do better.

Broad statements of purpose and vision capture important values, but vision statements by themselves are too abstract and ungrounded for specific action. The combination of purpose and vision statements (for example, strengthening communities and families) with specific, measurable outcomes (for example, reducing the incidence of child abuse and neglect, elevating high school graduation rates, or moving families from welfare to work) gives participants and communities a good way to measure success and makes the work tangible, real, and accountable.

THERE MUST BE NO BLAME, NO SHAME, AND NO ENEMIES

A key ground rule for the self-governance dialogues is the avoidance of blame. If something is not working as it should, report it and seek help to make it better. Blaming one another and those who are not present (for example, the head of a particular agency, a conservative or liberal political coalition, the state or federal government) benefits no one, least of all the community and its families.

The second ground rule is the avoidance of shame. We must be willing to speak candidly about what we know and do not know. A sense of humility is essential if we are open ourselves to new learning. We must be willing to admit what does not work and be open to changing it.

The third ground rule is that we create no enemies. We must stop blaming one another. When we do so we externalize our own power and control. Our focus must be on what we have responsibility for and control over. It is not productive to blame others for our situation. It gets us nowhere. Self-governance dialogues are about taking responsibility for our behaviors and those things over which we have influence.

In honoring these ground rules, participants are encouraged to use "I" statements only, not "you" or "they" statements. By emphasizing each individual's responsibility to contribute and a collective responsibility for overall outcomes, dialogues focus on identifying where we are, what works and what does not, and moving ahead.

SELF-MANAGED LEARNING IS ENCOURAGED

Community dialogues employ representative self-managed work groups throughout the session. By focusing on specific tasks and introducing elements of fun and creativity, (for example, notions of plumbing and replumbing the educational or welfare system), participants are engaged and hierarchy and power differences are minimized. In Ladysmith, Wisconsin, the county sheriff was down on his knees beside a dairy farmer, a child welfare worker, and an abused wife mapping the workings of the community's attempts to reduce domestic violence. In Pocatello, Idaho, the mayor was cutting and pasting pieces of pipe to create a picture of the community's programs for reducing child abuse. Participants discover, learn, and develop new or renewed relationships and ways of thinking by working on common purposes and tasks with a representative community group. In an open process where information is shared, mistakes acknowledged, and success celebrated, participants are more likely to commit themselves to meaningful action plans and goals.

VALUES AND BELIEFS THAT IMPEDE CHANGE MUST BE UNCOVERED

It is relatively easy to get communities and families to identify behaviors, funding decisions, and organizational systems and structures that need to be changed. It is harder for them to meet head-on the values and beliefs that undergird those dysfunctional behaviors and systems. Uncovering the values and beliefs that impede change is often the key to obtaining more effective outcomes for communities and families.

Maya Angelou put it well when she said, "It's very hard to agree to give up things you've known all your life: attitudes, positions, conceits. You will wonder, Dare I, dare I really lay this down? Dare I really give over the idea that women are really quite fine, but not as important as a man?" Giving up sexism, racism, or treating bureaucrats as the one-dimensional heartless enemy requires that we reveal and address our underlying beliefs and attitudes toward one another.

> Change is difficult. It is very hard to agree to give up things you've known all your life: attitudes, possessions, conceits.
>
> MAYA ANGELOU

Workers or citizens who believe in their gut that public service cannot be excellent do not expect excellence. In fact, they prevent excellence from happening. The adoption worker who believes that an autistic child is unadoptable will fail to make the extra effort to find those special parents who will adopt and love such a child. The state official who believes that communities cannot solve their own challenges will work to recategorize federal programs at the state level. Central to such beliefs is a lack of trust in the ability of individuals and communities to govern and organize themselves and a cluster of related values and attitudes that give rise to bureaucratic control-and-compliance approaches to change.

Self-governance dialogues attach faces, personal stories, and dreams to impersonal numbers, program structures, and expenditures. They reacquaint helping institutions, helping professionals, and those whom they serve with the community from which they receive financial, political, and moral support. They help celebrate common purposes and valued outcomes. Self-governance dialogues begin the process of rebuilding trust and faith in our communities and its social institutions.

SEPARATELY A PART; TOGETHER A WHOLE

Self-governance dialogues embrace a fundamental belief in the importance of the whole community engaged in the pursuit of common purposes and outcomes. That belief was corroborated by recent research linking community violence to values. Sampson, Raudenbush, and Earls (1997) found that individuals who were willing to get involved and take responsibility for their community made a crucial difference in controlling youth violence in the neighborhood. The presence of organizations and local services in a community were found insufficient. Citizen involvement based on collectively held values of trust was pivotal in asserting order in the community.

Community self-governance dialogues can help build a sense of collective efficacy in communities, organizations, and families. Collective efficacy is built one citizen, one neighborhood, and one program at a time. Experience with community self-governance dialogues points to the importance and power of trust, common values, and cohesion for achieving a community vision and outcomes. Everyone must be willing to do his or her part and to hold citizens and the community accountable.

What Appears Simple Is Hard

That which appears simple is frequently the hardest thing to do. Getting the lay community into the room, thinking outside the box, and securing leadership and follow-through are essential for the success of self-governance dialogues and community self-governance.

GETTING THE LAY COMMUNITY IN THE ROOM

As powerful as formal public and private systems are, they frequently are running scared. And the one thing that they are the most afraid and distrustful of is the community. They are afraid that, if they bring the community fully into the room, fully into a dialogue, they will be blamed and castigated for everything that is wrong with our communities and our families.

In fact the opposite is true. When the community is engaged in a self-governance dialogue, it understands more clearly the challenges families and service systems face. Communities come away from the dialogues with a new appreciation for the dedication and commitment of those who work with disrupted families and complex, equally dysfunctional systems. Rather than being the enemy, the community is a potential supporter and collaborator in efforts to strengthen communities and families.

THINKING OUTSIDE THE BOX

Formal systems do, however, have something to be legitimately anxious about. Although they need not fear that community purpose or community values will be at odds with their purpose and values, they should know that the community will push them to think and act outside the box. The community will ask why a family has to go to so many different agencies and tell and retell their story before receiving support. The community will ask why programs seek more money when they do not know how much money is currently in the system, where it is going, and what kind of return is being obtained for the investment.

At some point in a self-governance dialogue, many individuals begin to experience epiphanies. Service providers will begin to ask themselves, "What do these changes mean for me, my job, and my sense of security?" Citizens will realize how little time they spend with their children or how little they participate in the local parent-teacher association. A minister in a discussion about community literacy efforts will wonder whether all those parishioners who sit in front of him on Sunday morning can read their Bibles. If they cannot, he will ask, "What is my responsibility and obligation to help?" Thinking outside the box challenges people to consider how they themselves need to change to secure both the community's and their own personal vision and outcomes.

LEADERSHIP AND FOLLOW-THROUGH

Self-governance dialogues create both context and opportunity for distributed leadership and follow-up, but they do not guarantee either. However, leadership from the host organization and backing from community leaders, both elected and informal, do greatly improve the odds that the plan will be acted on and not shelved.

Self-governance dialogues model the concept of distributed leadership. Community members work side by side in shaping their understanding of a community system in education, welfare, and the human services. In the process, each has an opportunity to both lead and follow. For example, in Pocatello, Idaho, the mayor worked closely with a small group to devise new approaches to reduce child abuse and neglect in the community. Included in the group was a child protective service worker, a community volunteer, a teacher, and a young mother whose daughter had been killed by her father. Leadership rotates in self-governance dialogues as each individual applies his or her expertise and understanding to the tasks at hand.

In the end, whether there is community leadership and follow-up will depend on whether there is a conspiracy of good people, a saving minority, represented in the self-governance dialogue that will step up to the challenge. In most instances, these good people do step up. "Never doubt," as Margaret Mead said, "that a small group of committed citizens can change the world; indeed, it's the only thing that ever has."

CHAPTER 5

Day One: Building Community by Understanding the Present

Day 1: The Agenda

MORNING
- Host's welcome
- Community building
- Agenda at a glance
- A Sketch of the self-governance framework
- View from the leadership
- Identifying a common reality
- Performance gap
- Telling our stories
- Owning our outcomes
- 100-percent responsibility
- Present at the creation

AFTERNOON
- Moving forward by looking back
- Mapping the present
- Reporting

COMMUNITY VOICES Becky played with the picture frame in her lap. She lifted it up to her chest and then placed it down in her lap again. After a few seconds she repeated the process. The director of Idaho's regional health and welfare agency was finishing up his welcome to the assembled community group. He said that his child welfare staff could not be successful without the help of the community. He pledged that his system was open to changing the way in which it conducted its business. With the help and input from the community, he expected this day to signify a turning point that would lead to better results for the community's families.

It was her turn. She walked briskly to the front of the room. She did not appear to be nervous. As she moved to face the audience, she turned the picture frame over and pulled it tightly to her chest. Peering out from the frame was the face of a bright-eyed, curly-haired two-year-old girl, her daughter, Tanya.

Looking older and more more traveled than her nineteen years, Becky began to tell her story, a story she had told many times before. Her teenage husband Tom had shaken their daughter to death. He had been home watching Tanya while Becky was at work at a convenience store. The baby had not been feeling well and was crying a lot. He lost his temper. He picked the child up and shook her. Tanya died the next day from a brain hemorrhage. Tom said he had not meant to hurt Tanya, but he is in prison now. Becky is alone. She said that she hoped some-thing could be done to prevent this from happening to other children and parents. When she finished, she returned to her seat.

The Morning Begins

The morning of the first day of the self-governance dialogue begins with people streaming into a community center. The center might be at a church, community college, or the local YMCA, any place big enough to hold a large community group. It should also be a neutral site, unaffiliated with any of the dialogue's host organizations. Tables, each seating between eight and ten people, are arranged around the room to accommodate the expected crowd. There is an empty table in the center of the room to gather the proceedings from the dialogue that is soon to unfold.

Registration begins at 8:30 a.m. The community dialogue begins at 9:00 a.m. and continues until 4:00 p.m., with a forty-five minute break for lunch. Lunch is brought in for convenience and to ensure a quicker start-up afterward. The people pick up their registration packets and name tags. The registration packet contains an agenda for the two-and-a-half-day session, information on the outcomes that are to be the focus of the dialogue, and general information about the community. Earlier, participants received a letter of invitation and a personal call from the committee planning the event. The letter explained the purpose of the event, the vision behind the dialogue, and the outcomes that will be the center of everyone's attention. The personal call communicated to the invitee that his or her perspective and voice are needed.

People sit in mixed groups from the start to end. The tables have small folded tents on them indicating consumers, agency, school or organizational staff, and community stakeholders. The dialogue facilitators have placed these small tents at each table to capture the mix of people in each group. A large tent in the center of each table indicates which community outcome the group will be working on for the session. The outcomes have been identified in advance of the dialogue through conversations with representatives from the various groups hosting the event. There will be an opportunity to review, revise, and add new outcomes if needed.

HOST'S WELCOME

The day officially begins with the host welcoming the community to a unique event. The host may be a member of a community collaborative or steering committee or a representative of the sponsoring agency or institution. The host explains that the purpose of the self-governance dialogue is to gain the community's expertise and assistance in designing an action plan to secure particular outcomes for the community and its families. The vision and outcomes are presented. The members of the planning committee are identified and asked to stand if they are in attendance.

The host then introduces the facilitators. As outside consultants, the facilitators bring impartiality to the process. The self-governance dialogue is turned over to the facilitators and the assembled community. The facilitators explain that they will be leading the community through a highly participative and experiential process. The facilitators underline that they are not experts in the subject matter. Facilitators identify their role as uncovering the capacity of a diverse community to arrive at its own approaches to complex, difficult issues. All the expertise that is needed to improve results for families in the community is in the room.

COMMUNITY BUILDING

Several things are done at the outset of the dialogue to build a sense of community and familiarity among those in attendance. An icebreaker is used to introduce participants to one another and to demonstrate that everyone's expertise is needed to achieve the community vision. A sense of community is fostered by highlighting the diversity of the participants that come together for the dialogue. Participants also identify those who are still missing from dialogue and who will need to be engaged as the process moves forward.

THE LIMITS OF EXPERTISE

After the host's welcome, the facilitators engage the community through an icebreaker. The icebreaker is called the limits of expertise. At their tables, individuals are asked to think of a time when they were turned to as the expert in their families, communities, or workplace and to think about how it felt when, knowing that they did not have the necessary expertise, they went ahead and played the role anyway. After a few minutes participants are asked to introduce themselves and tell their stories to the group at their table. Each participant at the table introduces himself or herself to the group and tells his or her story. After all the stories are shared in the small group, the table is asked to tell one story from the group. The facilitator may begin the process by telling his or her own story.

Opportunities for participation are created when we individually are willing to acknowledge the limits of our own expertise.

One such story involves a newspaper reporter who called a facilitator about a story on welfare reform in the state. The reporter asked why a particular county in the state had recently declined an opportunity to set its own rules and eligibility guidelines for welfare reform. In a moment of self-congratulation for having been called on as an expert, the facilitator began to offer his opinion. It was not until halfway through the explanation that he realized that he had been trapped by his own hubris; he did not really know why the county had declined to volunteer. The facilitator backed up and suggested that the reporter call the county directly and speak either to the county manager or the director of the local welfare agency.

Sharing personal stories helps build a sense of relationship, engagement, and trust.

When reporting a story, the individual is asked what lesson he or she learned from the experience. For example, the facilitator learned, or perhaps more accurately, reminded himself, that he should speak only about what he knows. He should not speak for someone else. When he referred the reporter to others more knowledgeable, both the reporter and the public could get a more complete story of what is going on. To represent fully what is happening on any particular issue and at any moment in time, everyone's expertise and the voices of many parts of the community need to be heard.

WHO IS HERE

After all the participants have introduced themselves and told their stories, a list is posted on the wall of all the diverse community groups and voices that are in attendance at the dialogue. Showing the diversity present gives individuals in attendance a feeling that they are part of a bigger whole, a part of a concerned community. The process of sharing personal stories and the limits of one's personal expertise builds a sense of relationship, engagement, and trust both within the small groups and within the larger group, a sense that is built on and deepened throughout the session and continues when participants leave the dialogue.

WHO IS NOT HERE

After identifying who is in attendance, the audience is asked to identify who is missing. The facilitator makes the point that, if we are to secure the desired vision and outcomes for community and families, the whole community must be engaged, contribute to, and have a sense of ownership for what is going on. The voices and perspectives of business, religious, and civic groups, elected officials, the media, and ordinary citizens are needed to balance and expand the knowledge of representatives from formal helping systems. A list is made of those groups that are missing. The list is posted on the wall. Participants are invited to add to the list over the course of the dialogue. At the end of the dialogue, the group will return to this list and identify plans to bring missing community members into the process.

In the debriefing that follows this initial dialogue, facilitators focus the community's attention on its expressed intention of being inclusive in its self-governance. It is not unusual for dialogue participants to say they want inclusive participation but to let that commitment slide from their attention and actions. Facilitators, by drawing attention to it, provide a gentle goad for participants to act on that commitment.

THE AGENDA REVIEWED

After introductions are completed, the facilitators provide an overview of the two-and-a-half-day agenda. The morning of day one is devoted to introductions, gaining a sense of community, and exploring what we know about our community and its families. In the afternoon, current intervention strategies for securing outcomes are mapped out and reported on to the larger group.

Day two focuses on preparing ourselves to shift the way we think about our business and create a map of the future that will secure improved results for families and children. Day two closes by identifying personal commitments to change and setting the stage for action plans. Day three opens with action plans and concludes with a commitment to public accountability and a deepened sense of self-governance.

Table Roles and Ground Rules

Before the facilitators move to sketch the outline of the self-governance framework being used for the dialogue, they take a few minutes to outline the roles for the self-managed work groups at each table and the overall ground rules for the event.

TABLE ROLES

Each table represents a mix of consumers, citizens, and community and organizational stakeholders. Participants are drawn from a cross-section of relevant community and organizational networks linked to the identified community vision and outcomes. On each table is a large folded paper tent indicating the outcome the group will be working on. Small paper tents represent the composition of the group.

The facilitators request that each group of between eight and ten individuals takes a couple of minutes to assign roles to various members. These members help facilitate the management of their work for the next couple of days. Roles include facilitator, time keeper, recorder, and reporter. Facilitators are responsible for moving the discussion along and engaging everyone's participation. Time keepers maintain the schedule. The recorder is the scribe for the various group exercises. The reporter tells the group's story to the community assembled in the room.

SELF-MANAGED GROUP: ROLES WITHIN THE GROUP

Facilitator

Time Keeper

Recorder

Reporter

GROUND RULES

After all the introductions have been made, the agenda reviewed, and roles identified for the self-managed work groups, the facilitator goes over the ground rules for the dialogue. The ground rules are simple. There is no place for blame, shame, or enemies in community self-governance dialogues.

GROUND RULES

No Blame

No Shame

No Enemies

When discussing social change, individuals and groups frequently externalize problems. They blame, shame, and depict others as enemies. In doing so, they set themselves apart and above others in the community. In the process, they frequently alienate important segments of the community and disempower themselves. "We can't really tackle the court issues in child abuse cases because the district judge won't cooperate." "It is impossible to tackle school performance because the county commissioners will not allocate more money to the school district." "The public welfare agency can't ever do anything right."

There is no place for blame, shame, or enemies in community self-governance dialogues.

Individuals are advised to avoid blaming, shaming, or depicting others in the community as the enemy. They are advised to avoid using "them" or "they" statements and speak in terms of "I" and "we" statements. Each individual and group is encouraged to ask "What can I (or we) do with our knowledge and resources to be more effective? What can I (or we) do differently to engage those who are missing from this dialogue? And how can we move away from advocating against segments of the community whose support is needed to strengthen families? How can we join with all segments of the community to advocate for common purposes?"

Dialogue is encouraged and relationships are built when the parties are willing to be vulnerable, share what they know, and admit what they do not know. There is no point in shaming people for what they do not know, what they did in the past, or for being candid about their struggle to meet a particular challenge. Dialogue and trust are built when people identify the limits of their knowledge and expertise and ask others for their perspectives and help. The statement, "We need your help if we are to be successful" goes a long way toward building cooperation and interdependence.

A system that acknowledges that it does not have all the answers is taking the first step in a collaborative approach to securing a community vision. In a constructive dialogue, there is no room for good guys and bad guys, perpetrators and victims. For dialogue to lead to more effective practice in our communities, we must acknowledge that we are all governed by a common humanity, a general trustworthiness, and the desire to do the right thing by our families.

Facilitators will occasionally be called on to remind individual participants of the ground rules. When this happens, participants typically drop immediately any reference to blaming or shaming. Individually and collectively, they recognize that there is limited value in or gain to be had from such behavior.

SKETCHING THE PERFORMANCE FRAMEWORK

Having laid out the basic roles and ground rules for the self-governance dialogue, facilitators sketch out a framework that symbolically and visually captures the past and future of community efforts on behalf of families. The metaphor and the geometric shape of a diamond is employed to represent the basic elements of that framework. The term *diamond* conjures up both the image of a clear, strong gemstone and of the playing field for our national pastime, baseball. It acknowledges that most things that are precious are achieved through team effort.

Gemstones are created when intense pressure transforms a soft, opaque substance into a hard, clear crystal. Improving outcomes for communities, families, and organizations likewise involves a crystallization of community effort. In that process seemingly random and inconsequential efforts frequently join to produce the desired results. The baseball analogy comes into play because the figure that best captures the relationships between performance strategies and outcomes resembles a baseball diamond. Baseball games, like positive family results, are won not by individuals or individual programs but by teams of individuals and clusters of programs. Baseball games, like our efforts to gain positive results for families, are successful when team effort is allied with broad community support.

PERFORMANCE MAPS

In facilitating the performance dialogue, facilitators use the performance and outcome diamond (see figure 3) to help participants understand the process they are undertaking. The information on

FIGURE 3: **Performance and Outcome Map**

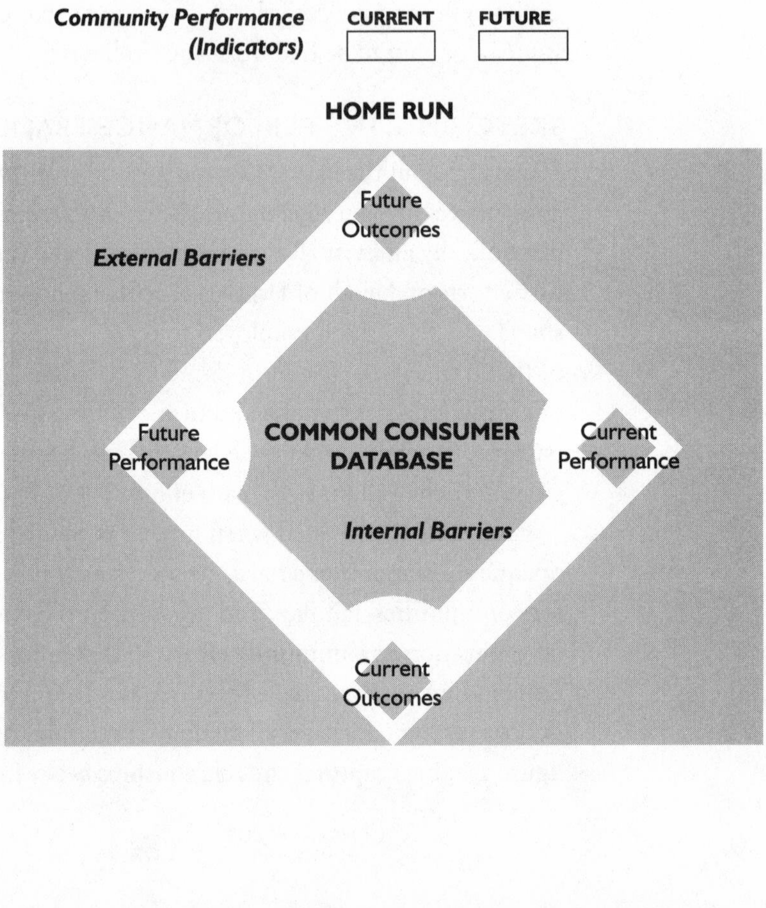

the diamond summarizes the relationships among outcomes and intervention strategies and sources of resistance mapped during the self-governance dialogue. A brief description of the various points on the diamond illustrates the point.

Above the diamond, there is a brief statement of community purpose along with present and future outcome indicators. The statement of purpose may be as broad as "securing a permanent family for every child" or as narrow as "relieving the stress of caring for a disabled child." Keeping score, tallying our outcomes, is aided by objective indicators of permanence in families or relief of stress for caregivers. Keeping score tells the community whether we are moving toward our specific goals and general community vision.

In the middle of the diamond itself, at the pitcher's mound, the common database represents everything we know, our best information about particular outcomes, the affected families, and the communities in which they live and function. Current and future outcomes appear at home and second base, respectively; at first and third bases are the community's current and future performance strategies. Performance strategies are the formal and informal interventions employed by the community to secure its outcomes. In the infield appear internal barriers to change; external barriers are in the outfield. Barriers may be located within the individual, family, organization, or community, or in the larger context of state and nation. They consist of a complex combination of tangible and intangible factors such as money, personnel, culture, and values.

The facilitators actually set up the room in the shape of a diamond and walk to each point on the diamond as they relate its significance. The physical layout of the room helps ground the diamond and community as team metaphor.

Once the community understands where it presently stands, it is asked a number of questions. How will it move to achieve a higher purpose marked by better outcomes? How does it move more families safely and quickly around the bases? How does it get more families home? How does the community protect, strengthen, and secure the home? When we map our present strategies for getting families safely home, we discover those approaches, related values, and assumptions that yield our current success rates. We know that if we are to do better, we need a new performance map that builds on what has worked in the past, reinvents new approaches, and identifies new values and attitudes that move even more of our families safely home. This new map is a guide to the future.

PERFORMANCE GAPS

Performance gaps are the differences between current and future success rates. The baseline is the rate of success in the current system. Whether we are talking about educational proficiency rates, the transition from welfare to work, or permanent families, it is important to acknowledge and build on the success that is in the system. For example, more than 65 percent of the children who were removed from their homes for child abuse and neglect in North Carolina in 1995 were either reunited with their own families or adopted within a year. Under its W. K. Kellogg Foundation child welfare reform initiative, Families for Kids in North Carolina raised the family permanency bar for itself, setting a goal of permanence within one year for 75 percent of the children removed from their homes.

CLOSING PERFORMANCE GAPS

Closing a performance gap begins with mapping the relationships between present and future outcomes and between present and future community and family interventions. When graphically presented, these paths represent our mental maps, maps that reveal the connections between intangible beliefs and values and tangible actions, structures, and services. They represent powerful images of how we believe the world does and should behave if we are to achieve positive results for communities and families.

View from the Leadership

By now, it is midmorning on the first day. The community-building exercise took perhaps half an hour to complete. The overview of the agenda and a sketch of the performance framework occurred more quickly.

The view from the leadership involves hearing from the host of the community dialogue and from consumers and families for whom the event is being hosted. The leader may be the director of the public welfare agency, the principal of a school, or the head of a family resource center. Families are represented by parents, students, welfare recipients, adoptive and foster parents, and adoptive and foster children. For example, Becky spoke for many parents when she conveyed her own story of family violence.

The intent is to have the heads of agencies, schools, or community collaboratives join with parents and children in giving voice to what they see as the purpose and vision of the self-governance dialogue. By placing these voices side by side, there is a leveling of the playing field between organizational leadership and citizens. A common vision is presented. The process of helping and being helped is humanized. Faces are to put to "systems" and "clients."

If parents and children are intimidated by the prospect of speaking to a room full of professionals, other parents, children, and citizens, the facilitators can ease the situation by conducting an informal interview at the center of the room. When the individual tells his or her story in the form of a personal interview, the presence of the other people in the room is temporarily blocked out. The citizens' voices are heard.

Involving consumers up front in the self-governance dialogue drives home a concept we call "nothing about them without them." This concept holds that a community should not plan or talk about families unless those families are in the room and participating in the dialogue. After the view from the leadership, the group takes a short break.

Identifying a Common Reality

After the break, the dialogue moves to establish a common reality. That common reality will inform subsequent planning and decision making. A common reality is generated from both objective secondary data and subjective personal stories linked to the vision and associated outcomes. This information comprises the common database, the information at the center of the performance diamond and at the heart of the self-governance process.

What becomes clear to the assembled participants as they begin to build a common understanding of the issues that they are dealing with is that each has only a piece of the whole story. Each has a segment of a complex puzzle. Only together can they assemble patterns that represent the whole story. Yet each of us, lacking an opportunity to build a common understanding, draws inferences and makes important decisions based on incomplete information. For example, some human services systems have no idea about the outcomes the current system generates and for whom. They can tell you about all the problems associated with families and the quantity and type of services they use, but little or nothing about their level of success. The implication is that well-intentioned actions, services, or teaching produce the desired outcomes: stable families and educated students. Their story is only part of the reality.

People also draw their information and inferences from more personal experiences. Personal stories have a powerful effect on an individual's perceptions and beliefs. Some individuals base their assumptions and decisions on the media's recounting of a single instance of abuse and neglect, mental illness, or welfare fraud. Others, working with families receiving assistance from the community, draw on their direct experiences. Still others tell their own stories of personal hardship and the receipt of help.

It is only when all these perspectives are laid side by side that we begin to have a sound foundation for making decisions that can profoundly affect the quality of community and family life. It is only after we have all the pieces of the puzzle that we begin to get a complete picture of what is happening to families in our community. It is only when individuals and the community as a whole begin to correct erroneous perceptions and assumptions that we gain a more common and informed understanding.

PERFORMANCE BENCHMARKS

An individual designated by the host begins the formal process of building a common database. The best quantitative information available is brought before the community. The information is drawn from local school or agency records or state information systems. From this information, current and future benchmarks are constructed for each of the outcomes under discussion.

Depending on the outcomes, the information may involve test scores for students, high school graduation rates, teen pregnancy rates, or the number of individuals moved from welfare to work in a certain period of time. Anything and everything that is known about results in the systems under question, what works with whom, where and when, is shared. For example, in a community seeking to improve family permanence, indicators such as entry rates into foster care, exit rates, and disruptions of placement while in foster care may be used. Patterns of entry, exit, and disruption from care are explored for different age cohorts and gender and racial groupings. Missing data are pinpointed. Facilitators remind the participants that there is no shame in identifying what we do not know. Plans are made to fill in the information gaps and move the group's understanding forward.

At times during the process, the host system will identify a good deal of useful (if previously untapped and unanalyzed) data. Other participants in the dialogue may add important pieces of information on the outcomes that they possess. All information shared with the participants in the dialogue is placed at the center of the room. These data and the personal stories to follow become the touchstone for the unfolding dialogue.

PERSONAL STORIES

Having begun to piece together a common database from existing records and data sets, the facilitators turn to personal stories to provide a qualitative and personal perspective on the family outcomes in question. Participants are asked to conduct an exercise called "prouds and not so prouds" with the people at their tables. They record on a piece of paper a personal story of something they did in relation to their table's outcome that they were proud of and, a second of something they were not so proud of. When they complete the task, they are asked by their table's facilitator to tell the group both of their stories. After reviewing the group's stories, participants share one of their stories with the assembled community. They are then asked to discuss what they learned from these stories and to share those lessons with the group.

Objective facts capture part of our common reality, but deeper meaning is often embedded in personal stories, not in verifiable facts (O'Murchu 1997). The personal story is at the heart of the scientific pursuit of knowing and the creation of meaning. Personal stories add context and moral voice to the act of knowing and discovery. By identifying what we are proud of, we stretch ourselves to imagine the possibilities for improving outcomes. By acknowledging the things we are not proud of, we assume responsibility for day-to-day realities that need to be changed. Our common reality is found not in numbers or personal stories, but somewhere in between. It is in between subjective and objective information that we engage in a process of seeking, knowing, experimenting, and discovering. A discussion of those things of which we are proud and for which we are sorry captures the struggle between knowing and doing. Our personal voice and experience, embedded as it is in an emotional, spiritual, and moral base, provides a narrative infrastructure that enlarges the heart, animates the spirit, and fuels our imagination of the possible. Personal stories are filters through which we translate incoming information and make sense and meaning of our lives. These personal stories are placed in the center of the room with the rest of the common data.

EVERYTHING THAT WE KNOW

Knowing is both a rational and an emotional experience. When we build a knowledge base for decisions, we consult the quantitative data, the research, and expert findings. We also consult our personal stories, our emotional and spiritual selves. It is through this combination of rational and emotional knowledge, the linking of the objective with the subjective, that the community's common reality is discovered. This platform provides the community with a foundation from which it can examine how it currently secures outcomes for its families.

The Afternoon Begins

The participants come back together after lunch with an emerging sense of community, an appreciation for what they know and do not know about the outcomes they are seeking for the community's families, and a sense of their role in creating that reality. Now they are champing at the bit. They are eager to get to work. For many participants, getting to work in the dialogue means shifting to a different learning medium. The morning's session is a mixture of didactic and story telling. By mid or late morning, facilitators will begin to feel the pulse of the group change as it becomes impatient to move to the task at hand. The afternoon and most of the next day and a half are occupied by experiential learning. The community will begin to simulate and experiment with reality itself. In the afternoon session, participants map and report on the present paths for securing outcomes for families in their community. In these visual, multidimensional maps, they identify what works and what does not work.

MOVING FORWARD BY LOOKING BACK

The most formidable barrier to creating a better future is the present. As uncertain as the future is, we are frequently not fully aware of how our present systems operate. Although we may have an appreciation for what we individually or programatically attempt to do on a day-to-day basis, there is seldom an opportunity to capture the way in which all the various parts, individuals and programs, come together. We are largely unable to articulate an understanding of the whole system.

To move forward, we must look back; we must examine and discover how our current communities, helping systems, and families work. How do communities, families, and systems come together to produce outcomes such as jobs for welfare recipients, permanent and loving families for children, and learning for students? Our understanding is aided by a process of simulation and play.

LEARNING IS DISCOVERY THROUGH PLAY

In *Play and Reality,* Winnicott (1971) demonstrated that the essence of learning is discovery through play. He observed that children simulate their worlds through the safe medium of toys. Toys serve as transitional objects through which the individual experiments with reality. The medium is safe because there is no way to win or lose.

In the self-governance dialogue, the real-life consequences of experimentation are momentarily suspended through the medium of mapping. Issues of trust and fear are put aside as community members come together to represent through a map or picture reality in their community as they know it.

MAPPING THE PRESENT

We are able to simulate the way communities currently seek outcomes for families through a process of mapping. Facilitators show the participants at their tables how to represent the ways in which their communities, families, and helping systems secure outcomes. In mapping the current system, the goal is to capture how that community system actually works, not how it should or ought to work.

Participants begin the process by brainstorming a list of all the various contributions and decisions that go into the system to secure current community outcomes. The list is compiled with no attention to order or the weight of each of the individual or programmatic contributions. In preparing for the mapping exercise, each table is given a length of butcher paper, a large envelope containing variously shaped pictures of plumbing pipe pieces, and a goody bag. The pipe pieces include multiple intake valves, various lengths of straight pipe, differently shaped elbows, and a spigot out of which comes a large drop of water representing the table's outcome. The goody bag contains bright paper streamers, small adhesive bandages, markers, stars, glitter, glue, and scissors.

The facilitators will often detect at this point, if not earlier, a measure of skepticism in the room. The participants are unsure whether they, as a group, will be able to capture the way in which the present system works. They are also just a bit skeptical about how pieces of plumbing pipe fit into a serious community dialogue. But they are patient and willing to give it a try.

Participants are instructed to take the pipe pieces and the goody bag materials and plumb their community system. The different lengths of pipe can be used to represent the time it takes a family to move though the system to an outcome (from welfare to work, for example, or from a child protective service investigation to a stable and more effectively functioning family). The pipe can represent all the inputs and decisions that transpire in preparing a child for learning in school. The different pieces capture the contributions of the individual, family, community, organizations, and associations. The variously shaped elbows represent the twists and turns that families and children experience in the community, both in its formal and informal helping networks. The goody bag materials are used to identify where things break down, where the flow is interrupted or diverted in unproductive ways. The Band-Aids mark the cracks and leaks in the network. Red crepe streamers mark bureaucratic obstacles and slow downs. Stars and glitter indicate where value is added in the journey to effective results for families. The pipes and goody bag materials serve as transitional play objects. They are employed to simulate how the present system does and does not work for families in the participant's community. Participants are able to suspend their distrust of one

another and their concern about making mistakes and engage in a
playful and entertaining simulation of reality.

They circle around the table or sit cross-legged on the floor discussing the current system animatedly among themselves. Parents,
program administrators, support staff, elected officials, and community volunteers position and reposition pieces of pipe on
the butcher paper. With colorful and playful indicators, they
begin to identify the leaks, cracks, and missing connections
in the community network. Some groups will mix their pipe
materials with their own art, creating shapes and lines that
capture their community's system. Creating maps, visual
pictures of the current community systems around each of
the community and family outcomes, participants are more
than pleasantly surprised at how well the exercise works. It
has brought them together as a group and community. It is
immensely educational and, not unimportantly, the process is fun.

Mapping our
present realities
through play and
art stimulates
our thinking and
learning. It is
also fun.

REPORTING

Facilitators move about the room checking in occasionally on the
working groups. Participants approach them for additional pipe
pieces or goody bag materials. Occasionally, a group appears to be
stuck, pondering all the pieces and materials strewn on the table
and not quite sure where to start. An individual may ask a facilitator for a point of clarification about the exercise. Eventually, after
some pondering, someone positions several pieces of pipe on the
paper. The others join in. Mapping the current system takes up to
half of the afternoon session. When the groups finish their maps,
they take a break for refreshments. With refreshments in hand,
they may return to put on the finishing touches. An air of content-
ment and completion begins to pervade the room.

Reporting findings to the assembled community takes the
remainder of the afternoon. In preparing their reports, groups are
instructed to begin to think about why their community systems
work the way they do. Asked to discuss among themselves the val-

ues or beliefs that hold the system in place, the participants brainstorm a written list of applicable intangible beliefs, values, and assumptions. Why do some children drift in foster care? Why are human services systems so fragmented? Why do families and children have to repeat their stories over and over again to various, overlapping agencies? Why do some schools have active parent involvement and others do not?

With their colorful maps and lists of assumptions and beliefs about what holds their current networks in place, the groups begin to report their findings. Some maps depict long, linear paths leading to the desired outcomes. Other maps reflect the twists, turns, and detours that families experience in navigating the community's complex networks of care. Some groups put the pipe pieces aside and create their own art, to map their community system.

Underneath the play is a serious purpose, an attempt to gain a better understanding of the world, the community networks, and the systems in which we live and operate. Underneath all the fun, learning is taking place. Individuals are learning more about the complex communities, systems, and networks of which they are a part. They are gaining an appreciation of how the various parts stream together to form a whole. As each group reports its story, the whole community begins to see and hear different themes and issues about what works and what does not.

It becomes clear that each group is dealing with many of the same families and interlocking issues. Parenting skills are linked to the prevention of child abuse and neglect. Education is linked to success in school. Success in school is linked to work. Work is linked to effective parenting. Substance abuse disrupts everything. The community begins to understand how success in each part is linked to success in other parts. The community begins to see itself as a team where every player has a part to contribute in a complex unfolding drama. The success of the whole—individuals, families, organizations, and communities—turns on the success and collaboration of the parts.

The First Day Ends

The first day ends in one last exercise. Each group places its map on the table in the center of the room with the rest of the common data and returns to form a circle. With the entire community standing in a circle and facing into the center of the room, the participants cross their arms in front them and hold hands with those on either side. The object of the exercise is to change positions so that everyone is facing inward but with arms uncrossed. The one rule is, however that in accomplishing this objective, everybody must keep holding hands.

A few moments pass as people ponder what to do. Unexpectedly, someone in the interlocking circle moves. Others follow. Then the group stops. Like a serpent folded over on itself, they are facing several directions at once. They are momentarily stuck. And just as unexpectedly, someone moves in another direction with a different solution to the task. People follow. After several false starts, everyone flows in a common direction. The circle comes to rest with everyone facing inward again.

The group applauds itself in a burst of collective energy. A brief discussion follows about what just happened. The group experimented with several different leads, reevaluated its position, and moved in other directions until it solved its task. All the while people held onto one another. There was some bumping, twisting, and uncertainty, and at times the process bordered on the chaotic. But no one let go. The community cooperated toward a common end and celebrated its success. In the end, each individual ended up standing in a different place. They all moved. They all changed. Everyone won. The group played and learned. The first day is officially over. The community breaks, ready to return the next morning surprisingly refreshed after a long emotional day.

CHAPTER 6

Day Two: Creating a
Bridge to the Future

Day 2: The Agenda

MORNING
- Creating a bridge to the future
- Overcoming our memories of the future
- Mapping the community's future

AFTERNOON
- Reporting future strategies
- Promises to the community
- The community stands in the gap

COMMUNITY VOICES "If there is one word that I would use to describe what is happening, it would be 'collaboration,'" said Paul Evans, a police commissioner describing his city's remarkable success in curbing youth violence. As of September 1997 no juvenile had been killed by firearms in Boston for more than two years. Boston's success in reducing crime, and that of other major U.S. cities, represents a marked shift away from the one-dimensional approaches to problems such as violence that hold that the police are responsible for controlling crime; the schools, for education; and welfare departments, for people who are poor. Boston's success in holding crime in check is, according to Chuck Wexler, the head of the Police Executive Research Forum in Washington, the result of an intense collective (multidimensional) effort by the police department, religious leaders, local community groups, and private citizens. "What is significant," he says, "is when you have an ad hoc community group in Kansas City, or the ministers' Ten Point Coalition in Boston standing shoulder to shoulder with the police in a particular neighborhood, saying this isn't simply a police problem, this is a community problem. That is what is most effective."

Jack Levin, the director of the Program for the Study of Violence and Social Conflict at Northeastern University, echoes the sentiment: "You can't evaluate in any quantitative way the contribution of the community vs. the policy vs. demographics vs. locking people up. But my sense is that in Boston it is the community members who have made the biggest difference" (Herbert 1997).

The Morning Begins

The second day of the self-governance dialogue begins at 9:00 a.m. Participants visit briefly with old and new acquaintances. Gradually they reassemble with their previous day's work group. The morning begins with a brief discussion about shifting one's mental map— the way we see and behave in our world—and an illustrative video clip. After the video and discussion, the work groups move on to the primary exercise of the morning, mapping new pathways for achieving the community's outcomes and vision for its families.

New explanations, mental maps and ways of working together accompany the process of social transformation.
PETER SENGE

Creating the Bridge

Self-governance dialogues, by fostering community learning, create a bridge to the future. Through a process of inclusive dialogue, the first emergent steps are taken into uncharted and unfamiliar territories. These steps and discoveries represent a qualitative change in direction for families, organizations, and communities. Transformation through dialogue is a part of a natural evolutionary process. As with each new journey into uncharted territory, the process of social transformation is accompanied by new explanations, mental maps, and ways of working together (Senge 1990), new ways of thinking and doing that constitute a paradigm shift (Kuhn 1970).

HOUSTON, WE HAVE A PROBLEM

A ten-minute video clip from the movie *Apollo 13* is used to illustrate how a community of individuals can respond effectively to a crisis. In the flight of Apollo 13, a crisis develops when the oxygen supply is threatened by a mechanical breakdown. The crew members, with the assistance of those on the ground, have a limited time to solve the problem. If they are not successful, they will perish. Failure is not an option.

The use of stories and metaphors, in this case a movie segment, engages the participants' understanding of essential points and principles in a way that an abstract didactic discussion cannot. The video enlists the emotions of the participants as well as their intellect. The mix of facilitation techniques used throughout the self-governance dialogues acknowledges that people are engaged and learn in different ways. The following lines from the video illustrate a process whereby participants in the room begin to think about shifting their own approaches to solving community problems.

By saying "Houston, we have a problem," the Apollo 13 flight crew acknowledges its predicament. In a similar vein, unless participants in a self-governance dialogue acknowledge that they also have a serious problem, they will be unwilling to challenge their own thinking about how to resolve that problem. Boston residents have become more and more unwilling to tolerate the violence that has robbed them of their freedom and has stolen so many of their children. Liberals and conservatives alike recognize that the current welfare system robs many families and children of both their freedom and their future. Dialogue participants must feel a sense of urgency about securing the outcome at their table. Failure must not be an option.

"Wake up anybody you need. Let us work the problem. Let us not make it worse." As the Apollo flight and ground crews tackle their common challenge, the problem-solving process is opened up to anybody who might be able to make a contribution. From that point on, the mission is to get the crew home safely. The mission is no longer to go to the moon. The original flight plan is put aside. The chief measure of success lies in looking at what things *can do* rather than what they were designed to do.

Self-governance dialogues engage anybody and everybody who is needed to tackle the problem successfully. Communities, through self-governance dialogues, work the problem. They are careful not make the problem worse. In the same way that the Apollo 13 crews simulated, improvised, and experimented with creative solutions to their problem, community self-governance dialogues simulate, improvise, and experiment. They continually mold and remold new and different approaches to securing the community's vision of itself.

There is growing agreement that reliance on simply arresting people without involving the community can make the problem of crime worse. The police come to be seen as an occupying army. Law enforcement officials across the nation are acknowledging that, to combat crime effectively, they need the community and the community needs them. The mission is no longer just to arrest criminals. The mission is to reduce crime. Arresting criminals and putting them in jail is only one part of a more complex collaborative approach to reducing crime. Likewise, self-governance dialogues foster multifaceted approaches to complex problems. In Pocatello, Idaho, the community, in examining the issue of youth violence, pointed to the lack of constructive recreational outlets, such as community pools, teen centers, and work opportunities. A coalition was formed to establish a family resource center to help address the gap.

OVERCOMING OUR MEMORIES OF THE FUTURE

Strong communities and families are the product of successful adaptation to changing social and political environments. Successful adaptation involves effective community learning.

Piaget (1986) observed that there are two types of learning, assimilation and accommodation. Most of us are most comfortable with learning by assimilation: taking in new information, placing it in recognized structures, and ascribing meaning in relation to those structures. We fit new information to our current mental maps. Learning by accommodation demands much more of us. It is both an experiential and intellectual process by which we adapt our own beliefs, ideas, and values through an interplay with others holding different beliefs, ideas, and values. It is a creative process. It is a process of discovery in which new pathways, behaviors and attitudes, and mental maps are forged.

Those who learn by assimilation frequently operate from what de Geus (1997) called "memories of the future." In our desire for certainty, we fit new information into known receptacles. Traditional planning does not usually mean anticipating and constructing new futures but rather building memories of the future from familiar and safe assumptions. People's desire for certainty and predictability is so strong that we will act against our better judgment rather than create something new and incur uncertainty and risk. Partial change is achieved when sweeping change is needed.

Through the medium of self-governance dialogues, families, organizations, and communities learn by accommodation. Participants are able to perceive new signals in a changing social and political environment. Through dialogue and the process of accommodation, they are able to challenge, modify, strengthen, and change various internal beliefs, ideas, and values. They are able to live with the uncertainty that accompanies the creative process of adaptation and change. Learning by accommodation is an experiential unfolding of both the intellect and the heart. Although they are unaware of what the end result will be, they do know that they will be different for having gone through the process (de Geus 1997).

Mapping the Community's Future

It is midmorning. Participants are eager to get on with the work of designing their future and creating new ways of working together to secure improved outcomes for families. They will work on their future mental maps all morning. A break is taken when the individuals or work groups need it. The goal is to complete the maps by noon when they will have lunch on site. Maps are reported on after lunch.

BEGIN WITH THE END IN MIND

In beginning the process of mapping future pathways to community outcomes for families, the work groups at each table are instructed to start at the end and map backward to free themselves of the tendency to project their memories of the future—the way they have always done things—onto their maps of the future. Looking back over the maps they created the previous day, the groups are able to identify what works and what does not work in the current system. In thinking about the future, they discard what does not work and build on what does. They create something new if unfamiliar.

Before the work groups begin constructing their new maps (using new sets of pipe pieces and goody bags), they are asked to review their lists of the beliefs and values that hold dysfunctional aspects of the current system in place. They will have to overcome many of these beliefs and practices if they are to construct new ways of collaborating and working in the community. For example, educators may be at a loss for ways to partner with the business community. Nonprofit family services agencies often see the public child welfare agency as an enemy that seldom does right by the community or at-risk families. Others may never have envisioned social workers working directly with police officers on community policing teams. Still others may have never thought of stationing central office social services staff out in neighborhood family resource centers.

Having reviewed past beliefs and practices, participants are asked to brainstorm a list of new approaches and strategies that reflect the promise of improved outcomes for families. This charge is exciting. It taps into their creative selves. It presents them with the opportunity to discuss approaches they have always wanted to try. It asks them to stretch their imaginations. Individually and collectively, they have always known better than they have done. Now they have a forum and an opportunity to build a new and different future for themselves, their families, and their organizations and community.

PRESENT AT THE CREATION

Traditionally, when social systems are designed or redesigned, most of the people affected have no part in the design or redesign. The system is built outside their presence by the usual suspects, high-level administrators, policy analysts, and planners. The design and associated recommendations become someone else's model. There is little compelling about such plans for either those who are to implement them or for those who are to be served by them (de Geus 1997). There is little sense of collective ownership for either the plans or the visions.

People feel ownership and responsibility for what they have a hand in creating.

In contrast, the simulation of system designs or redesigns through a process of group mapping fosters new collaborative mental models. It captures the interaction, diversity of perspectives, and intuitive reflection that is essential to challenge the familiar and create the new. The pieces of pipe serve as transitional objects that help participants shift from one way of working with communities and families to another. Participants experiment with reality and put new ideas and suggestions for action before the group. They modify them through dialogue. And then they commit them to paper. Being present at the creation of system designs and redesigns helps the community secure for itself ownership of both the change process and its final products.

MAPPING THE FUTURE

What emerges from this creative process are maps to the future in the form of replumbed community and organizational systems. These maps of community and organizational systems are characterized by greater flow, more timely routes to securing family outcomes, and a circular, replenishing feedback process. The maps are the product of extensive community and organizational collaboration.

Pipes are shortened and straightened as red tape is peeled away. Duplicative steps are eliminated. Overall communication is enhanced. Leaks are fixed as the links between the family and community—its schools, media, the religious community, police, and helping institutions—are coupled together; relationships are adjusted and tightened as needed. The contributions of the various sectors of the community join to create an ever-mounting flow of energy and commitment. The maps created by many communities come to look less like long linear systems and more like looping, winding, and ultimately circular pathways. Results in one area replenish the energy, approaches, and results in another.

The Afternoon Begins

The morning session breaks for lunch on a noticeable high. Clusters of participants worked feverishly to complete their maps of the future before noon. Some groups continue to work during lunch as they tie together the remaining loose ends. Others use the time to network with old and new friends alike, reveling in the opportunity to explore new collaborative partnerships. The large community gathering is nourishing to both the heart and the intellect.

In the afternoon the participants will focus on reporting on the various community maps and sharing new strategies and beliefs. The maps will serve as a jumping-off point for action planning beginning with individual promises to the community.

REPORTING FUTURE STRATEGIES

A little blurry eyed and sleepy after a hectic morning and big lunch, each group is requested to bring its map to the head of the room and report the story behind it. The maps, many of which are festively and imaginatively decorated, spark fresh energy back into the room. Each reporter, with assistance from his or her group, is asked to provide a step-by-step accounting of the group's recommendations for improving the outcome for which it was responsible.

At the end of each account, the groups are asked to identify some of the new beliefs and values that inform the process they have just outlined. When they complete their reports, they place the maps at the center of the room with the rest of the community's common data.

NEW STRATEGIES AND APPROACHES

With their eight- to ten-foot maps of replumbed community and organizational systems suspended in front of them, each group reports its recommendations to the assembled community. The groups identify where strengths in the current system have been built on and where new approaches have been plumbed into place. Questions are taken from the audience both to clarify and at times modify the group's recommendations.

In Alamance County, North Carolina, the community looked to build on the strength of recent community prevention initiatives. Using these efforts, it sets about the task of redesigning traditional approaches to financing child welfare so that prevention approaches can be supported. One program it wanted to strengthen was a newly established volunteer respite program for at-risk families. Families experiencing difficulty in parenting and whose children are at risk of abuse and neglect are able to call on neighborhood families to provide an afternoon or a weekend of respite. Parents have access to information on effective parenting skills and other family support services as needed. The goal is to help prevent abuse and neglect by providing respite and strengthening family parenting skills.

IDENTIFYING NEW BELIEFS AND VALUES

Dialogue facilitators ask each community, as they did in Alamance County, North Carolina, to identify the beliefs and values that accompany their newly designed approaches. Again the point is made that, unless the community and its central organizations can overcome certain beliefs and values about how things are to be done, their recommendations will be stillborn. The beliefs and values that lie below the surface of the statement "That is not the way things are done around here" are among the most formidable barriers to change.

In Alamance County, participants observed that efforts to strengthen prevention approaches to child abuse and neglect ran headlong into the traditional practice of using public money almost solely to pay for investigations of abuse and neglect and foster care placements for children. Strengthening prevention approaches, the community observed, requires both a shift in

attitudes toward prevention followed by greater financial investments in front-end prevention services. To this end, Alamance County chose to experiment with a national waiver for Title IV-E foster care dollars. That experiment allows for investments in prevention services in return for the promise of future reductions in the number of children in foster care. The community has agreed to take that risk.

Promises to the Community

Having reported on their maps of the future and identified some of the values and beliefs accompanying new ways of doing things and working together, the group members take a refreshment break. They have earned it.

When the participants return, the self-governance dialogue moves to an exercise called "promises to the community", commitments to action and learning that individuals in the self-governance dialogue make of themselves and request of someone else in the community. The promises are made in the name of securing improved outcomes for families. Community promises involve the assumption of 100-percent responsibility for personal actions and requesting the assistance of others to achieve a common purpose.

The facilitators turn each group's attention to a sheet of paper in the self-governance dialogue information packet. The top of the sheet reads *Promises to the Community*. Each participant is asked to complete the sheet, date it, and sign it. The exercise contains two parts—two promises. First, participants are asked to identify what action(s) they personally will promise to ensure the group's success. Second, participants are asked to request a specific action or assistance from someone else or some organization in the community to support the outcome in question. Participants complete this exercise at their tables. When everyone is finished, the facilitators ask for volunteers to read their promises to the community. Several individuals volunteer.

The facilitators draw on the examples presented by the various volunteers to illustrate the importance of individuals assuming personal and collective responsibility for action. Although the maps of the future represent an energy and excitement associated with new paths to the community's preferred vision of itself, it takes individuals walking those paths and leading the way to turn that vision into reality. Each individual's promises to the community are placed at the center of the room with the community's common data.

100-PERCENT RESPONSIBILITY

Self-governance is something dialogue participants must model. Participants are asked to "be the change they want to see in others." It is not just something that they can talk about doing. It is not just an abstract concept. It involves assuming 100-percent responsibility for personal action. It involves dialogue participants behaving and learning their way to a common purpose.

The first step for responsible action begins with each dialogue participant. Self-governing communities, organizations, families, and individuals extend their potential and secure their common purpose by taking one step at a time, modeling first personal responsibility and then collective responsibility. Each decision is followed by action and then new observations about the effects of that action; then another step is taken (de Geus 1997). Each new step outlined in the self-governance dialogue, each new direction that it charts for itself, is informed by the conditions of the moment. Change is a continous learning process fed by multiple converging streams. Many paths feed that sense of common purpose. There is no one single path. Life, according to the poet Machado, is a path that we all beat as we walk it. Self-governance and walking the talk is not something that we can externalize or assign to others.

In demonstrating personal responsibility, we ask ourselves to be the change we want to see in others

In Greenville, South Carolina, a young minister made a promise to his community that he would set up a literacy group in his church. He wanted to be sure that everyone in his congregation could read the Bible and participate fully in the economic and social life of the community. In Ladysmith, Wisconsin, a representative from the local department of social services made a promise that he would assist the community in developing a proposal to establish a family preservation program. In Burlington, North Carolina, a citizen volunteered one afternoon a month of his time to provide transportation to any family that needed it.

For every act of individual responsibility, there is the promise of significant change. If every minister assumed a measure of responsibility for the literacy of his or her congregation, if every public servant reached out a hand to his or her community to assist in the development of an innovative initiative, and if every citizen promised an hour or two a month in service to the community, all these individual and seemingly inconsequential grains of sand—human action—could trigger an avalanche of change.

Complexity theorists refer to this process as the butterfly effect—small and seemingly insignificant events such as the movement of a butterfly's wings yield large changes at distant points. The warming of the ocean water by a couple of degrees in the late summer off the coast of Africa can spawn unpredictable and devastating hurricanes on the coast of North Carolina thousands of miles away. The actions of individuals, seemingly small and inconsequential by themselves—a parent taking more time with a child, a neighbor acting as a child's mentor, or an adult volunteering in his or her neighborhood school—can yield, after many years, a healthy productive adult who contributes to his or her family and replenishes the life of the community.

REQUESTING THE ASSISTANCE OF OTHERS

Openly sharing information about yourself or your organization and your successes and failures models a willingness to be vulnerable and an openness to learning and change that is contagious. Openly sharing information also earns individuals and the community the credibility and right to ask for assistance from one another in redesigning processes that do not work. Self-governance dialogue participants, after making a promise of personal action on behalf of their community, request a promise of assistance from a representative from the community, an individual or an organization to set the process right.

Requests for assistance and for changes in current behaviors and attitudes are informed by the community's maps of its current systems. It is through these maps that community secrets and shortcomings are made public. The maps identify where the process breaks down, where action is delayed, and where ultimately care and justice are denied. Much akin to the process of revealing family secrets in therapy, revealing community secrets about system dysfunctions is an important first step in a healing process. When community secrets are acknowledged and talked about in an open and frank dialogue, the air is cleared of misinformation and misunderstanding. The stage is set for assigning responsibility without attaching blame.

An open and participatory dialogue uncovers an interdependence between individual acts of responsibility for self and collective acts of responsibility and accountability to one another. Self-
governance dialogues emphasize a holistic conception of social
responsibility that consists of two interdependent halves, responsibility for self and assistance to others. Tocqueville (1990) referred
to this intertwining of responsibility for self and others as "self-
interest rightly understood."

When a community maps the paths to improved educational
outcomes, it identifies parental involvement as a central contribu-
tor to children's educational success. Community maps also identify one of the major barriers to that success as inflexibility in the
workplace. In the name of improved educational outcomes for the
community, dialogue participants ask the business community or
a particular company to support parental involvement with their
children through a more flexible workplace. When a community
maps the paths to ensuring child safety, it identifies the termina-
tion of parental rights of abusive and neglectful parents as one of
those paths. The same community map will also point to the child
welfare worker's difficulty in making such weighty decisions on his
or her own. The worker and his or her agency may be open to the
suggestion that they join in a broadly based community assessment team, one that includes the family, to make and stand by difficult decisions when necessary.

Promises to the community illustrate the importance of both
self-evaluation and self-responsibility and community accountability and community responsibility. Self-evaluation and self-
responsibility model the principle that change and responsibility
begin at home with the individual. Community accountability and
community responsibility acknowledge that social transformation
and change is an interdependent collective process.

Responsible parents need to invest time and energy in their
child's education but they also need the support of their workplace
to enable them to attend school meetings and care for a child when

he or she is sick. If child welfare agencies are going to make and stand by difficult decisions, they need the commitment and expertise of child welfare workers but they also need the support and assistance of an involved community.

A COMMUNITY STANDS IN THE GAP

Self-governance dialogues capture a community's vision of its present self and what it aspires to be. They identify the gap between who we are and who we would like to become. They identify those actions, beliefs, and values that underlie our present behavior and they point us toward the future by way of a map of emerging behaviors, beliefs, and values. Self-governance dialogues engage the community voice in all its diversity to help us secure that future and our common community purposes.

A community that makes and keeps its promises to its families is a self-governing community.

Self-governance dialogues place communities and families at the center of the debate about who we are and who we dream we can be. Through self-governance dialogues, communities acknowledge that there are many paths for achieving what are broadly common purposes. These paths are as diverse as America itself. They are both liberal and conservative, religious and secular, public and private, and as ethnically and culturally diverse as the rainbow. A community that makes and keeps its promises to its families is a self-governing empowered community.

The Second Day Ends

It is nearing 4:00 p.m. The day is drawing to a close. A great deal has been accomplished. The community has challenged itself to shift the way it thinks about working with families. It has challenged itself to open up to new approaches, attitudes, and values that will yield marked improvements in community and family well-being. The community has met the first part of the challenge.

Maps outlining comprehensive and diverse strategies for securing outcomes for families have been developed. And through the exercise of promises to the community, the group has embarked on a personal and collective process of action planning.

Tomorrow, participants will return for a final half-day session to prioritize their strategies, draw up initial action plans, and develop a plan for public accountability and follow through. They are exhausted but pleased. The facilitators suggest that they give themselves a hearty round of applause for a good day's work. They do so happily.

CHAPTER 7

Day Three: Community Ownership and Accountability for Results

---

Day 3: The Agenda

MORNING
- Prioritizing community initiatives
- Reviewing maps and promises
- Prioritizing outcome strategies
- Creating a community action plan
- Community performance teams
- Community self-governance and and public accountability

COMMUNITY VOICES Several people leaned forward to examine the spreadsheets on the table. It was rare to see so many help-ing professionals interested in numbers. Everyone seemed to be talking at once. On one spreadsheet, the number of children entering foster care in Iredell County, North Carolina, was compared with data from the rest the counties in the state for the years 1992 through 1997. It was exciting to see that their county had broken away from the state trend. Fewer children were entering and staying in foster care in their community.

Martha Cox, the coordinator for the community's Families for Kids performance team, watched and listened to the discussion with much satisfaction. She had been in child welfare for many years. This was a new day. Group discussions of child welfare caseloads and particular cases used to be a covert activity in the agency. The discussions never reached into the community. The workers and the agency were expected to handle troubled families on their own.

Now line workers, supervisors, employees of related service agencies, interested community advocates, and family members met to discuss particular cases and overall trends in foster care placement. The collective sharing of information and learning together was beginning to pay off. Families in their community were being strengthened, and kids were being kept out of foster care. Children who were already in foster care were being adopted or reunited with their families more quickly than ever.

A social worker rapped his knuckles on the table and called the meeting to order. Margaret Cox started the meeting with a report of the last quarter's performance. They had definitely turned the corner in their community. Results continued to be favorable. The performance team was proud that it could demonstrate results for the community and its families.

The Morning Begins

It is the third and last day of the community self-governance dialogue. As the 9:00 a.m. start time rolls around, it is clear that the group has thinned a bit. Family members, business representatives, elected officials, and other participants from the community at-large find it difficult to get away from their regular lives for two and a half days. Even so, a core group of system representatives and a healthy number of community participants remain. They take their seats. They are ready to get down to the specifics of what happens next.

The last session of the self-governance dialogue is devoted to prioritizing action steps for each of the community and family outcomes and to identifying initiatives and strategies that affect those outcomes. Individual work groups will prioritize actions specific to their outcomes. The group as a whole will identify overlapping themes and strategies.

Having prioritized specific outcome strategies and cross-cutting themes and strategies, the facilitators sketch out a community action framework to help the work groups break down their broadly stated strategies into more discrete actions and indicators. The morning concludes with three activities involving the group as a whole. A sign-up will be held in the middle of the morning to establish a community performance team. It will be followed by a discussion of the role of self-governance and public accountability and the identification of the community body that is to be responsible for governance. If such a community self-governance group is unavailable, the performance team will play a dual role until one is established.

Prioritizing Community Initiatives

A facilitator greets the participants. Their energy and commitment to the community and the self-governance dialogue is acknowledged. This last morning is identified as the time when the rubber begins to hit the road. Each work group has laid out broad strategies for reaching its destination. Now, the groups must prioritize their strategies and begin to lay the foundation for specific actions and follow-up.

REVIEWING MAPS AND PROMISES

Each work group is asked to take fifteen minutes to review its maps to the future and its promises of individual and collective action. The groups are asked to develop a list of the major strategies represented in their maps and promises. When they have compiled that list, they are asked to prioritize among themselves three steps for immediate action.

Some groups retrieve their maps from the common data table at the center of the room. Others rifle through the stack of community promises at that table to refresh their memory of what it is that they promised of themselves and requested of someone else in the room. Other groups begin immediately to discuss the various strategies and promises related to their family outcomes.

PRIORITIZING OUTCOME STRATEGIES

Surprisingly, the groups prioritize their three strategies for securing their family outcomes rather quickly. Arriving at consensus is easier among participants who have discussed, ruminated over, and cut and taped their way to a new future over the past two days. One or two groups may take a little longer because of the presence of a wordsmith in their midst. Most settle comfortably on broad statements of strategy, leaving the final wording to those who will pull together the final report and determine the next steps after the dialogue.

A facilitator calls time. As each group reports its recommended strategies, a second facilitator records them on the flip charts placed around the room. At the top of each page, the group's community and family outcome is written. Under it are the group's three strategies. After each report is given, questions and requests for clarification are taken. There is little debate or disagreement over the various suggestions. Each group's prior reports on present and future strategies have clearly provided a solid base of understanding of central issues, vital concerns, and the impending shift in direction.

IDENTIFYING CROSS-CUTTING STRATEGIES

As the group reports go up on the flip charts for everyone to see, several common themes and patterns begin to emerge. Calls for improved communication, greater collaboration, more accessible information on what works, greater involvement of families and the community, and feedback on results echo in a number of the group reports. Participants are at once surprised and reassured by the commonality of issues and recommendations.

A facilitator asks the whole group to take a couple of minutes to look at the reports and identify three strategies that cut across the various outcomes. Then the facilitator asks the group to identify those common strategies or themes. For example, many communities identify the need to develop comprehensive community assessment teams and flexible financing. With each suggestion, the facilitator goes around room to the various flip charts to see whether that strategy came up in that particular group. If it did, it is circled. Within a very short time, three strategies are identified that cut across the various community and family outcomes in the dialogue. These are recorded on a separate flip chart.

Creating a Community Action Plan

Having prioritized strategies for both specific and cross-cutting community and family outcomes, the facilitators now challenge the groups to do something quite difficult. They ask the groups to begin the process of translating lofty vision, outcome, and strategy statements into action plans at the community and organization level. They are provided with a Community Action Plan Framework to assist them. The framework is a modification of Kaplan and Norton's (1996) work on strategic management systems and balanced scorecards and Robinson and Robinson's (1995) work on performance consulting.

Self-governing communities move from vision to action.

Each group is provided with a legal-size spreadsheet showing the Community Action Plan Framework (see figure 4). At the

FIGURE 4: **Community Action Plan Framework**

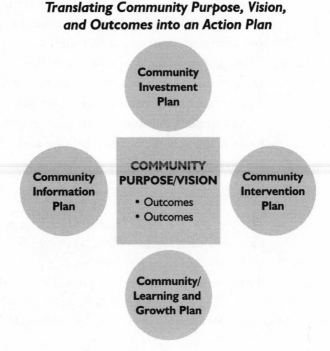

Translating Community Purpose, Vision, and Outcomes into an Action Plan

Community Investment Plan

Community Information Plan

COMMUNITY PURPOSE/VISION
- Outcomes
- Outcomes

Community Intervention Plan

Community/ Learning and Growth Plan

center of the framework is community purpose and vision, followed by outcomes and indicators of success. Surrounding purpose, vision, and outcomes are four strategy dimensions comprising a community action plan: interventions, investments, learning and growth, and information. When communities and organizations act on their purpose and vision, their action statements become an integrated set of objectives, indicators, performance targets, and strategies that identify who is responsible for discharging and overseeing each activity.

PURPOSE, VISION, AND OUTCOMES

When filling out its action plan, each group focuses on its general statement of community purpose and the specific outcome it is working on. Each and every proposed action is ultimately assessed in terms of whether it helps the community achieve its vision and outcomes. Each component of the plan—interventions, investments, learning and growth, and information—must be interwoven in a way that helps secure long-term measures of success.

In Alamance County, North Carolina, the community self-governance dialogue had as its common purpose and vision "strengthening communities and families." The outcomes that it set as measures of success were reduction of the number of children in foster care, reduction of the incidence of substance abuse among families, reduction of the incidence of child abuse and neglect among families, and improved access to health care for at-risk families.

INTERVENTIONS

The work groups, having restated their common community purpose and outcomes, move quickly to specify each of their four action plan components. The first component involves identifying the community interventions proposed to secure each group's outcome. The group identifies the objective associated with each intervention strategy, indicators for that intervention, performance targets, and who is responsible.

The Alamance County work group that focused on reducing the number of children in foster care identified community assessment teams as an intervention strategy central to its approach. The objective was to provide a comprehensive community assessment for children at risk of being placed in foster care. A performance indicator is represented by the scheduling and holding of weekly team meetings. A performance target for community assessment teams is the assessment of 100 percent of those families for whom there is a report of abuse and neglect. The team will be coordinated by the county department of social services and will include representation from community service agencies, families, and citizens.

LEARNING AND GROWTH

Community learning and growth is the second action plan component. This component identifies areas of learning and growth necessary to support specific community interventions and secure identified outcomes. In opting for a community assessment team approach to reducing the number of children in foster care, Alamance County pointed to team training as essential for participating community system, family, and citizen representatives. A performance indicator in this area is the achievement of identified competencies in team process. The overall performance target involved providing training and achieving team competencies for all team members. The University of North Carolina's Jordan Institute for Families was identified as the community partner that could provide training for the community assessment teams.

INVESTMENT PLAN

The community investment component of the action plan asks dialogue participants to think about the financing implications of the proposed intervention plan. Participants are encouraged to think of financial plans as investment strategies that are measured by return on results.

Continuing with the Alamance County example, the community investment plan makes provision for financing the community assessment team. The plan combines the contributions of participating community agencies and the host agency, the local department of social services. The financing of the team is linked to community's overall strategy of reducing the number of children in foster care.

The objective behind this component of the community investment plan is to use the money saved from decreased foster care placements to support prevention services such as the community assessment team and family support services. Success is indicated when funds are secured for the team, linked to the reduction in children in foster care, and savings invested in family support and prevention services. Lead responsibility for this portion of the community investment plan is shared by the local department of social services and a community governance task force.

INFORMATION PLAN

The information component of the community action plan ties all the various action elements to the long-term indicators of community success, its common purposes, and outcomes. The general objective of the information action plan is to make connections between the various components of the action plan and community results evident. The community performance team and local department of social services assume responsibility for the information action plan. Linked information systems are the linchpin of system and community learning. They provide an indispensable feedback loop between actions and results. Outcome-based information systems help answer the question of whether, when we put all our strategies and related actions in place, we can expect to find the changes we desire for our communities and their families.

As the groups work on their community action plans, the facilitators move around the room answering questions. Some groups struggle with the challenge of moving from broad statements to detailed local action. The action plan worksheets help. Participants are encouraged to be as specific as they can on their action plans, but not to worry. Work groups such as the community performance team and staff within the host dialogue organization(s) will follow up their efforts and add the necessary detail. With their community action plans initiated, the groups take a midmorning break.

Community Performance Teams

After returning from the break, facilitators send around a sign-up sheet for the community performance team. Membership consists of key staff from the host organization and a representative cross-section of the community, including lay citizens and family members. Community performance teams and team members are responsible for discharging a complex set of community and organizational responsibilities. They are responsible for forging the next action planning steps, overseeing ongoing planning, and engaging in process of continuous self-evaluation and learning. Together, action planning and self-evaluation constitute a new empowerment approach to community-based initiatives.

ACTION PLAN ROLE

A facilitator moves to the center of the room and stands next to the common data table. With a sweep of the hand, she indicates that the performance team will be responsible for taking everything that the community knows about itself, its vision, its desired outcomes, and its fledgling action plans and creating a report that outlines the next steps in the community's quest to shape its future. The report will represent an evolving blueprint of the community's dreams and commitment to action.

The facilitator indicates that she will be available in the weeks following the self governance dialogue to facilitate a debriefing session. The action planning role is ongoing and linked to the development of a capacity for self-evaluation and self-governance. Through this linkage, planning becomes a dynamic, unfolding process characterized by experimentation, evaluation, feedback, and learning. Action planning is a learning process where the traditional steps of strategic planning, implementation, and evaluation are collapsed into one continuous process at the community and organizational level.

Community self-governance is a continuous process of learning and adaptation.

SELF-EVALUATION ROLE

The community performance team, in conjunction with its action planning role, is responsible for an ongoing evaluation of the community's progress toward its outcomes and common purpose. It is responsible for tracking progress on action plans and key community outcome indicators, and providing feedback to the community and relevant organizations.

The community performance team operationalizes its organizational and community learning through a mix of evaluation and program monitoring methods. It monitors key process and outcome indicators, employs surveys and questionnaires as necessary, and conducts qualitative assessments through citizen and consumer focus groups. The community performance teams report findings and recommendations to both their host organization (such as the local child welfare agency or school) and a community self governance task force (such as consortium of families and children or an educational partnership).

ENSURING INCLUSIVE PARTICIPATION

The performance sign-up sheet wends its way around the room and eventually returns to the facilitator who calls out the name of each volunteer. Volunteers identify their role in the community (as, for example, agency administrator, family member, elected official). Their names are written on a flip chart. When all names are listed, the facilitator observes that certain groups are not represented on the performance team (for example, the business and the religious communities are missing). A pitch is made for representatives from those communities. A few additional hands go up and names are added to the performance team. The volunteers are asked to stay a few minutes after the self-governance dialogue ends to set a date for a follow-up debriefing session.

Community Self-Governance and Public Accountability

The last items on the agenda for the day and for the dialogue concern community self-governance and public accountability. An open discussion format is used. The facilitators outline issues associated with self-governance and public accountability for results. A case example and framework for thinking critically about self-governance and public accountability are presented and discussed with participants.

In communities that possess self-governance structures for families, community performance teams pass on their findings and recommendations to these bodies. Performance teams provide analysis and recommendations specific to various community initiatives, dialogues, and outcomes. Community self-governance bodies are typically responsible for steering the array of community-based initiatives that affect families. Governance bodies may range from educational partnerships to welfare reform collaboratives or proponents of juvenile justice initiatives.

Community self-governance bodies possess both a broad community vision and the formal and informal authority necessary to move specific community initiatives forward. They are able to place the specific action plan recommendations associated with the various self-governance dialogues into the larger community

context. They are able to engage the power and influence of community as a whole, facilitate the overcoming of barriers to change,
and serve as a central sounding board for general and specific
community concerns and accountability. Where such bodies are
absent, community performance teams play the dual role of performance team and self-governance entity until a broadly based
self-governance structure can be developed.

The facilitators acknowledge that the placement of this item at
this point in the dialogue is somewhat unfortunate, given that the
participants' attention spans are beginning to slacken. The facilitators also acknowledge that, in many communities across the nation,
broadly based self-governance structures are only beginning to take
shape. Self-goverance structures in various communities are at very
different stages of evolution. Overheads outlining a self-governance
framework and a case application are provided to participants. The
handouts help the participants to think about the topic both in the
last session and in the days and weeks after the dialogue.

A CASE EXAMPLE

Developments in Georgia in recent years provide a good illustra-
tion of self governance and public accountability. The state is
actively evolving a complex interwoven system of state and local
governance for families and children. As observed earlier in the
book, a Policy Council for Children and Families has been put in
place at the state level. At the local level, community partnerships
are being developed. The state council is responsible for strategic,
results-based decision making, resource baselines, and outcome
benchmarks. The Policy Council seeks to establish a fiscal accountability system that links results with funding decisions. The council
and community partnerships work hand in glove to bring about
improved results for families.

Local community partnerships are responsible for community
partnership agreements, result and budget accountability, and self-
evaluation. State and local self-governance are centered around

twenty-three benchmarks that tap into areas such as child health, readiness for school, school success, and strong and sufficient families. Georgia communities are striving to build private, public partnerships to secure valued results for their families and communities.

Community Governance as a Learning and Adaptation Process

Community self-governance is defined for dialogue participants as a loosely coupled process of community learning and adaptation. The framework that is used captures the larger community context that determines and shapes community and family outcomes. The framework draws again on the work of Kaplan and Norton (1996) on strategic management and balanced scorecards for business. It modifies their work to fit the concept of community self-governance for families.

The self-governance process and framework centers around easily accessible, comprehensive information about communities and their families (see figure 5 on the following page). The information is presented through comprehensive community scorecards that rate the community's fitness on a number of different family and community dimensions. They also signify a decision to hold the community and its key institutions publicly accountable for the well-being of families. The scorecards are at the center of four interdependent community learning and adaptation processes. The four legs that anchor this process include stating and translating community purpose(s), communicating and educating the community, intervention planning, and feedback and learning. Community and family self-governance takes place in a context of learning and adaptation involving families, citizen associations, private and public helping systems, the media, businesses, the religious community, and elected officials. Community scorecards provide a public means for keeping track of our progress.

FIGURE 5: **Community and Family Scorecards**

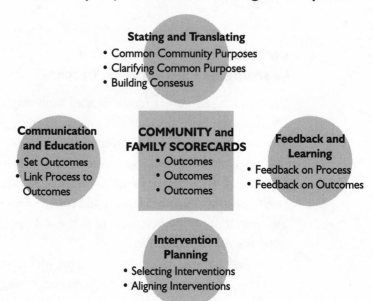

Community Self-Governance, Learning and Adaptation

Stating and Translating
- Common Community Purposes
- Clarifying Common Purposes
- Building Consesus

Communication and Education
- Set Outcomes
- Link Process to Outcomes

COMMUNITY and FAMILY SCORECARDS
- Outcomes
- Outcomes
- Outcomes

Feedback and Learning
- Feedback on Process
- Feedback on Outcomes

Intervention Planning
- Selecting Interventions
- Aligning Interventions

COMMUNITY AND FAMILY SCORECARDS

The scorecards provide communities and families with a reflection of their progress relative to their stated common purpose(s) and the progress of other communities and in the state. Georgia's Policy Council for Children and Families believes that accountability for results is fundamental to improving the lives of families and children. The results framework represented in the concept of scorecards challenges communities to be innovative, collaborative, and creative in securing improved outcomes for communities and families.

Georgia, to continue the example, is pursuing a series of outcomes for its communities and families. One set of outcomes is grouped under the goal of strengthening families. Strong families in Georgia are reflected in the following outcome indicators: a reduction in teenage repeat births, reductions in the incidence of child abuse and neglect, increase in the percentage of children in foster care who are placed in permanent homes, and reduction in the percentages of juvenile arrests.

An additional outcome in this area is evaluated through a new family index that measures the increase of stable families. Stable families are defined as those in which the first birth is to a mother who has completed high school and is age twenty or older and where the father's name is recorded on the birth certificate. Counties in Georgia are able to compare themselves to similar counties using these and other benchmarks.

STATING AND TRANSLATING COMMON PURPOSE(S)

The first leg of community and family self-governance is the identification of common purposes that all segments of the community can agree on. Stating a vision or purpose(s) that most people in the community—liberal and conservative—can agree on establishes important common ground for a process of collective action. Building consensus around those purposes is essential for effective collective action.

The Georgia Policy Council's vision statement is just such a statement of common purposes. It reads: "The vision of the Policy Council is for Georgia's children to be healthy, start school ready to learn, perform better in school, and have stable, economically self-sufficient families. Georgia's hope is for all of its children to grow up to become productive, contributing members of society."

COMMUNICATION AND EDUCATION

The second leg of community and family self-governance is communication and education. The driving assumption is that an engaged and educated public will rouse itself to secure necessary changes for its communities and families. A public that has easy access to information concerning the well-being of families can be trusted to act on their behalf.

Georgia developed its framework for improving results for families and children through a year-long deliberation among state and local leaders and citizens. The council and its emerging community partnerships represent a cross-section of the state's citizens. The council has plans for working with all 159 of Georgia's counties and their citizens.

INTERVENTION PLANNING

Intervention planning is the third leg of community and family self-governance. It involves selecting and aligning community interventions that will yield positive results for families. Through a process of widely shared information about what works and what does not work, the self-governance process stimulates prevention services, system reform, collaborative planning, local decision making, and creative local control of finances.

Cecil M. Phillips, the council chair, expressed the community's demand for more effective approaches to solving Georgia's difficult community and family problems. "It is no longer sufficient to talk, we must do! Despite more than thirty years of the best intentions and a great deal of money, state and federal programs have achieved unsatisfactory and unacceptable results. Our entire society is at risk if we do not fix the problems in this state. The council is ready to partner with communities and families to ensure steady improvements in child and family well-being, and to link resources to results."

FEEDBACK AND LEARNING

The fourth leg of the community and family self-governance process is feedback and learning, which is central to every self-governance framework. Real-time processes are needed to identify those private and public interventions that add value to communities and families and those that do not. Communities need to retain and build on what is valuable and discard or redesign what is not.

Georgia, through its local community partnerships, is emphasizing community-driven decision making that brings citizens and organizations together to identify what works best in their communities and weave those practices into a comprehensive system of private and public support. Like many states across the nation, Georgia seeks to wrap communities around families with the support and assistance of the private and public service sectors.

Community Ownership of Outcomes and Public Accountability

The last step in the self-governance dialogue involves a brief discussion of community ownership and responsibility for outcomes. Facilitators use the analogy of a United Way campaign drive to illustrate the concepts. When you drive across the country and enter small and large communities alike, you will frequently encounter a red and white thermometer. The thermometer tracks the community's progress toward meeting the goal of raising a specific amount of money to support local community agencies and programs through its United Way campaign. Everyone recognizes this sign as a community's commitment to its citizens and the citizens' commitment to their community.

Public ownership and accountability for results places a necessary creative tension on a community, its institutions, and families.

Public accountability for positive results for the community's families needs to be as easily understood and recognized. Whether it is a thermometer in front of the community's high school tracking progress toward an identified graduation rate or a thermometer in front of the welfare agency tracking movement from welfare to work, the results must be publicly recognized and supported. Public accountability and ownership of results places what Peter Senge (1990) refers to as a "creative tension" on the community, its institutions, and families. It is a creative tension that stimulates us to learn from our successes and failures. It prompts us to reinvent ourselves continuously in pursuit of improved results for our community and its families.

If participants in the community dialogue return responsibility for change, learning, and results to the experts after the event ends, a critical source of accountability will be lost. With government and private institutions, the public must continue to participate in an ongoing process of community adaptation and change. Self-governance and public accountability is the right and responsibility of all members of the community to contribute to the process of improving outcomes for families.

The Self-Governance Dialogue Ends

The last session of the day elicits many questions and suggestions about the self governance framework and public accountability. It stimulates discussion among participants on what was happening in their community. But there is also a clear, almost palpable feeling in the room that it is time to wrap up the self-governance dialogue. Myriad questions, points of clarification, and "what ifs" will have to wait for another day and a subsequent self-governance forum to be voiced, perhaps in the community performance team meetings.

Several participants stand up and begin to say good-bye to their table mates, by now true partners in a common venture. A facilitator and representative from the host organization hold up their hands and beg one last indulgence from the audience. Someone has created a colorful banner with the community's vision emblazoned on it as a slogan: Families and Communities Working Together. There are several small tubs of finger paint on a table. Participants are asked to dip a hand into the paint, made a handprint on the banner, and sign their names. When they are done, they proudly hold the banner up in front of them as someone snaps a picture.

A small group of concerned citizens is now captured on film, their deeds to be duly reported in the resource center's newsletter. With a little paint under their fingernails as a reminder of their work and camaraderie, participants file slowly out of the room, committed to continue the process they have begun.

Democratizing Governance and Management

To maintain the momentum achieved through community dialogue, social institutions and programs must turn that energy and commitment into new ways of seeing things and working together. Social institutions and programs nourish and grow new relationships and partnerships when they share the process by which they learn, make decisions, and hold themselves accountable.

In this last section of the book, I identify the principles and assumptions that underlie our further democratization of governance and management. I identify tips for shared learning, decision making, and creating a common culture of self-governance at all levels of society. I outline both a structural and cultural context in which citizens, guided by common purpose, can successfully shape a brighter future for their communities and their families.

CHAPTER 8

Putting Shared Learning and Accountability into the System

COMMUNITY VOICES It had been an intense but exciting two days. Nearly two hundred people had convened in Athens, Georgia, for a dialogue on child safety. It was a diverse gathering. The conference room at the First Baptist Church was packed. Families, concerned citizens, social services staff members, representatives from the print and broadcast media, teachers, mental health professionals, and business, religious, and community leaders gathered for a common purpose, preventing child abuse and neglect in Clarke County. A local radio station has set itself up outside the conference room.

The first day opened with a welcome by the new director of the county Division of Family and Children. Only two days earlier, she had been the mayor of Athens. The dialogue also opened with a presentation from a young woman whose children had been removed from her custody. She had not been able to control her alcoholism. Both women shared a common vision, protecting children. Both struggled with the difficulties of making decisions so that children would be safe and families strong.

As the dialogue began to wind down on the afternoon of the second day, the groups reported their strategies. One group tackled a barrier common to many human services initiatives: How does a community decide whether efforts at ensuring child safety and well-being are working? The group reported strategies designed to capture the information necessary to answer that question. One strategy included developing a new evaluation partnership with the University of Georgia. Other groups followed with their recommendations. It was clear that timely, local accountability mechanisms would be essential for community learning and success.

The dialogue ended with a cross-section of community representatives volunteering for a community self-evaluation team. The team would put in place assessment and accountability strategies to help steer the community's approach to child safety and well-being. The community had engaged the challenge of preventing child abuse and neglect. People left the Baptist Church hopeful and energized.

Returning to the Real World

People leave dialogues with a renewed sense of purpose. They make new relationships and entertain perspectives that they had not been exposed to before. There is a feeling that their community is coming together. There is a real sense of optimism and possibility in the air. Each person reflects on changes he or she can make in his or her private and public lives. Participants make promises to the community to hold themselves accountable.

This is not an uncommon feeling. We have all been there. Yet when we return and settle back into our real worlds and routines, we find it difficult to keep up our focus, energy, and commitments. And when we push for change, even small changes, we run into a wall, a "push back" (Senge et al. 1999). The push back originates in our organizations and communities. Part of it originates in ourselves. It is hard to make a break from old ways of seeing and doing things. It is hard to break old patterns and create new ones. Part of the reason that it is so difficult to change ourselves and our social institutions is to be found in the way in which we learn and think about evaluation and accountability. Unfortunately, the ways in which we usually evaluate and monitor both ourselves and our social institutions discourage participatory learning and change.

To maintain the momentum initiated by a community dialogue, we must reframe assessment and accountability as a shared and open learning process. The momentum and energy necessary for change can be maintained by creating participatory forums and learning opportunities in our home settings. A process of shared learning and accountability must be placed into our social institutions.

Barriers to Thinking Differently about Learning and Accountability

Virginia picks up her child from day care in the late afternoon, returns home, and prepares a quick meal. She has to work that evening. She will have to drop her child off again, this time at her mom's place.

When she thinks back on her recent assessment meeting with the welfare worker at the social services agency, it makes her angry. It seems as though the social workers do not appreciate how complex and difficult her life is. It feels as though they are trying to control rather than help or care for her and her child. They assess her but they do not really ask her what she wants. They do not seem to listen or understand. It feels as if something is being done to her rather than with her.

When directors, principals, top program managers, researchers, line teachers, and social services staff members return to their offices from dialogues, they also return to complex and busy lives. They are besieged by a host of pressing matters. When they think about accountability and evaluation, their first thoughts do not typically involve reflecting on their own behaviors and actions. They do not typically think about how they and their programs might manage their own learning and change differently. Evaluation and change are typically directed at others, not at themselves.

For local programs, an evaluation usually means that the federal or state government comes in to do a financial or program audit and evaluation. In a similar vein, when schools and human services programs assess and measure families and students, these families and students feel as though something is being done to them rather than with or for them (Usher 1995). Traditional assessments, evaluations, and testing methods at all levels reflect a generally adversarial, detached, "us versus them," simplistic approach to change and accountability. It is not something that you willingly do to yourself or for yourself. The process is neither participatory nor shared. It adds little value to either your learning or your work.

Learning and accountability begin with self-assessment.

The professor returns to campus after the community dialogue to finish up an evaluation report. He feels a little uncomfortable being so directly involved in a social program. He is more comfortable holding himself apart from programs, their staffs, and their consumers. He feels it keeps him objective. Although he wishes everyone well, he does not feel personally attached to the success of the program. He is uncomfortable sharing his information with the program or anyone else until the final report is written.

Management and line staff members from schools and mental health, juvenile justice, and family services agencies return to their separate hectic worlds. The connection experienced in the community dialogue is hard to maintain. Each person is held accountable to different funding streams, laws, and regulations. The fact that they deal with many of the same families and children and overlapping issues does not unite them in the way that it should.

The minister, the small business owner, the neighbor, and the concerned citizen all return to their separate, busy lives and schedules. They have few direct experiences with human services or education. They are not sure of what their responsibilities are or should be in relation to the community's social institutions.

Accountability and learning in both the community and its social institutions are fragmented. Each of us assumes responsibility for only our narrow part. Few of us understand how our part fits into the whole. Few of us accept responsibility for the whole.

Traditional accountability and evaluation measures foster competitive and adversarial relationships within and between helping institutions and the community at large. Measures simplify what is in fact a complex world. The focus is on external regulation and control rather than on internal self-regulation and self-control. Traditional approaches to learning and accountability have the effect of further isolating and dividing family and community interests. They engender an air of personal and professional detachment. They do not foster mutual learning and accountability.

In summary, there are five barriers to reclaiming one's own reflective self-assessments, learning, and shared accountability:

- Limited awareness

- Divided interests and accountability

- Competitive and adversarial relationships

- Simplicity and external regulation

- Claims of detachment and neutrality

Principles for a Shared Learning Process

Lynn Usher, a professor with the Jordan Institute for Families at the University of North Carolina at Chapel Hill, puts up the first overhead for the community performance team. The overhead tracks children as they move through foster care in the community. It points to a couple of trends. The lengths of stay for children in foster care have decreased over the past three years. But the population remaining in care is older and is more likely to be male and minority.

Dialogue, reflection, and shared learning challenge each of us to do better. The following five principles provide us with direction in thinking about how to create structures and practices of shared learning and accountability in our social institutions:

- Learning and accountability begin with self-assessment.

- Learning and accountability are based on shared interests.

- Learning and accountability are cooperative.

- Learning and accountability are self-regulating.

- Learning and accountability involve the creation of personal meaning.

BEGIN WITH SELF-ASSESSMENT

Dr. Usher asks the team members, who represent a cross-section of the community, what they think is going on. He purposely resists offering any opinion or analysis. A lively discussion breaks out. People offer additional pieces of missing information. The community analyzes its own data, and it explores different reasons that some of its children are remaining in foster care.

Each party to the discussion reflects on his or her contribution and understanding of the process. Participants share that self-assessment. They contribute what they know. As the discussion moves back and forth, a collective knowledge begins to emerge. The group is able to piece together an understanding of the whole from an assessment and reflection on all the parts. The process of reflection and self-assessment begins with oneself—the agency director, line staff member, the young mother, and the external evaluator. It is a nested process. It begins with the individual and extends to the family, system, and community.

A BASIS OF SHARED INTERESTS

Learning is a participatory process founded in shared interest and accountability. No one party has either all the knowledge or a sufficient frame of reference within which to assess various contributions and perspectives. Learning assumes a shared interest between the party assessing itself and others. Learning transcends any one perspective or contribution to understanding.

Learning and accountability are based on shared interests.

Those involved in the learning process may include family members, neighbors, members of the religious and business communities, and stakeholders in the policy and practice community. Shared interests and accountability provide a mutually agreed on backboard against which to bounce understanding and derive meaning. All the involved parties are united in a desire to do their part and see positive results (Usher 1995).

COOPERATION

A shared interest in outcomes calls for participatory reflection and cooperative learning. Team-based approaches are better able to generate important insights in the design, implementation, and evaluation of social interventions. Team-based learning enables us to make the necessary, real-time, midcourse corrections. Through a process of continuous cooperative reflection, approaches and interventions are shaped and reshaped.

Learning and accountability are cooperative, not adversarial processes.

An environment, whether it is a family, organization, or community, that honors reflection and learning nourishes new ideas and supports change. In such an environment, the playing field becomes more level. The power of learning and the creation of meaning are shared. Respect for innovation is communicated. It is a democratic environment in which all parties are open to the influence of other people and ideas.

SELF-REGULATION

Shared learning and accountability trusts the capacity of people from diverse backgrounds to direct their own learning. It honors a deep internal need in each of us to direct our own learning and creativity. And, because it honors that need, it taps everyone's talent and contribution to an adaptive process of change. Although self-regulating learning processes stimulate creativity, they are also often chaotic and messy. They ask us to respect the inclusiveness and diversity. They ask us to go slow in order to go fast.

To learn and create new understandings and ways of doing, one must be willing to tolerate and risk failure. One must be willing to live on the edge. Living on the edge and falling off occasionally are integral to the creative process. Learning and change are not for the faint hearted.

THE CREATION OF PERSONAL MEANING

The first thing that runs through most people's mind when faced with change and a demand to learn new ways of doing things is "What does this change mean for me? Will it help me or harm me?" Learning and change are intensely personal. By creating opportunities for people to participate in creating new understandings and meanings, the fear of change is addressed. By creating opportunities to participate in the creation of new understandings and meanings, people can take a hand in uncovering what works and what does not work and shape new ways of proceeding. People own the understandings and new meanings they have a hand in uncovering and creating.

Tips for Shared Learning and Accountability

How can we create such an environment? How can we better support ourselves and others who return from dialogues and discussions with fresh ideas, excitement, and energy? Principles of shared learning and accountability help. They provide a lens for seeing social institutions, communities, and families in a new light. The principles offer a framework for sorting and selecting new approaches and interventions that sustain and build momentum for change. They provide each of us with a conceptual map for overcoming barriers to change and forging new directions. The following tips and strategies draw on these principles. They build a common foundation of understanding that fosters self-governing decision making and empowerment.

RELENTLESS FOLLOW-UP ON RECOMMENDATIONS

Perhaps one of the best ways to maintain the momentum for change is relentless follow-up on personal commitments and group recommendations. The minister in Greenville, South Carolina, who follows up on his commitment to bring literacy education to his congregation is a good example. The director of the family resource center in Wisconsin who follows up with the local department of social services on requesting resources to plan a family preservation program in her community is a good example. Trust and support are built when we follow through on our commitments.

In 1994, Mayor Rudolph Giuliani appointed William Bratten to the job of Police Commissioner for New York City. Bratten encountered a restive public, a somewhat demoralized police force, and Giuliani's promise of safer streets. He immediately reorganized management and shifted to strategies focused on results. But what earned him the most credibility among line officers and the public was that he listened to them and followed up (Harvard Business School 1996).

In the first week on the job, Bratten followed up on what he heard from interviews with officers on the street. He pushed for automatic weapons, improved bulletproof vests, and darker, more authoritative uniforms for his officers. He also took disciplinary action against those officers who stepped out of line. Officers felt that he went to bat for them. He followed up on their requests for change.

He hired a consultant, John Linder, to assist him in collecting data on which to base action. He mapped crime where it was happening and developed strategies that made a difference. Officers concentrated more on neighborhood and community needs. In the period between 1993 and 1995, New York City registered a 25.9 percent drop in crime. Other major cities in that same period averaged a 5.4 percent reduction.

THE TOOLS FOR SELF-ASSESSMENT

Providing tools for self-assessment and learning is essential if results for communities and families are to improve. Under Bratton, regular CompStat Meetings with precinct offers were held to map, track, and report crime statistics. What got reported, measured, discussed, and supported got done. Previously, information was not organized, analyzed, or fed back into the decision-making process. The meetings teased out what was happening and why. They pooled diverse perspectives on common information.

The commissioner provided the necessary tools and technology to get on top of crime.

Family support and family resource centers are a fast-emerging field of early intervention and prevention services for families. Many of these programs are grass roots in nature, long on heart and sometimes shorter on management and self-assessment skills. The Family Resource Coalition of America, after thorough discussion with field and test pilots, offered a program self-assessment toolkit for the family support field called "How Are We Doing?" Using an easy-to-understand format, assessment data is stored on a computer. Once inaccessible information and technology are made accessible, understandable, and usable. Communities, organizations, and families benefit when we provide them access to tools, technology, and data to inform their decision making and self-management.

CLEAR OWNERSHIP OF OUTCOMES

People take care of what is theirs. When people either own something directly, such as a home, or experience responsibility for a behavior, such as parenting, they are more likely to behave responsibly. Likewise, when teachers, child welfare workers, or community members are invited to participate in self-evaluation and decision making in their community, it becomes their process. They step up to the plate. Linking an individual's accountability and decision making to ownership and responsibility for those decisions motivates people to do their best.

The U.S. Department of Housing and Urban Development in 1993 developed a program called Family Self-Sufficiency. The program is designed to help Section 8 public housing residents become homeowners. Residents sign a contract with explicit goals such as maintaining suitable employment and remaining off the welfare rolls. As they reach their goals, money that would normally be lost to rent is contributed into an escrow account for the family. As a family meets its goals, it can withdraw money from that account to buy a home or use it for education or to start a small business. If the family does not meet its goals, the money reverts to the housing authority. By building assets, something that is their own, these families create a sense of future possibility.

PARTNERSHIPS IN ACCOUNTABILITY

When we create shared accountability in a family or community for its own well being, we tap into our desire to be part of something larger than ourselves. We also provide a public place where we can contribute our talents and gifts. People are motivated by a desire to contribute to their family, workplace, and community.

Learning and accountability involve the creation of personal meaning.

In Savannah, Georgia, the Chatham-Savannah Youth Futures Authority employs a participatory approach to evaluation and learning that is part of a larger community development strategy. It is characterized by partnership and shared accountability. Metis Associates, a New York–based evaluation firm, was engaged to guide local capacity for participatory self-evaluation. The firm employed a mix of qualitative and quantitative self-evaluation feedback methods to support an evolving array of integrated family support services. In taking this approach, Metis Associates honored the Greek origins of the concept of *metis,* the "art of locality." It speaks to the wide of array of practical skills and knowledge that arise in a given context to address and learn from a particular challenge. It is reflective of context and culture. Metis, a local partnership of shared accountability and creation, possesses the capacity and flexibility to make adjustments and overcome barriers specific to that context.

FOLLOW-UP ON MISSING INFORMATION

Reflection, learning, and accountability are only as good as the information they are based on. Often, good information and data are missing. Providing for follow-up on missing information helps sustain the impetus for change.

Clarke County, Georgia, home to Athens and the University of Georgia, has the resources and skills essential to the generation of good information systems. In the Athens community dialogue, Family Connection, a local governance group made a commitment to follow up with the University of Georgia to capture missing information on how the community was doing in the area of child safety. The group made a commitment to begin to develop a longitudinal database to track how families and individuals were doing in the community on the issue of child abuse and neglect.

LAVISH COMMUNICATION

W. Edwards Deming held that 97 percent of what matters in an organization such as a school, or for that matter a family, cannot be measured. Much of what is in fact measured and monitored in our social institutions is a misuse of our time. Bureaucracies tend to evaluate and measure what they can control, measures of presumed quality and intervention standards. They evaluate policy manual rules and procedures.

Senge et al. (1999) observed that social complexity and social challenges are best met by mixture of simple measures, the 3 percent, and informal measures, intuitive self-evaluation and self-regulating conversations, the 97 percent. Crime statistics, graduation rates, and prevalence of abuse and neglect all are meaningful measures to which we should hold ourselves accountable, "How are you doing?" and "Is it working?" and "Why not?" These measures are the 3 percent. They provide a practical and contextual measure of how we are doing. In self-governing environments, people also learn from conversation and stories. The way we get things done is often less a matter of control and measurement than it is of trust, intuition, and open communication.

The 97 percent is measured in a simple, informal way with questions such as "How are things at home" and "How are your classes going" and "Do you have friends to talk over what is going on?" Much of the record keeping that prevents school counselors from working with students and child welfare workers from talking with vulnerable families should be replaced with more face-to-face contact and dialogue.

OPEN ACCESS TO INFORMATION

Learning and accountability flourish best in an open environment in which information is freely accessible. Whether you are talking about a family, an organization, or a community, inaccessible or incomplete information more often than not contributes to inaccurate inferences and poor problem solving. Developing structures and processes for openly sharing information is essential for strong families and a democratic society.

The Urban Institute, in a project called Assessing the New Federalism, helps communities analyze the devolution of responsibility for social programs from the federal government to the states. It does so by tracking shifts in health care, income security, and social services indicators. The information is available through an Internet site. The Annie E. Casey Foundation also makes state-level data available to the public, advocacy groups, and policy makers on the well-being of families and children through an online source called KIDS COUNT Data.

Increasingly, states are making available county- and community-specific data on the well-being of families and children. Both Oregon and Georgia have led the nation in benchmarking family and child well-being at the community level. The Children and Families Commission in Marion County, Oregon openly shares information with the community through publications and the activities of its Progress Teams, participatory community groups that track progress on a comprehensive set of community indicators.

The City of Los Angeles, with the nation's largest child welfare system, is creating a process for making data on results more accessible. With the assistance of the Annie E. Casey Foundation, the Jordan Institute for Families, and the University of California at Berkeley, information will be made available to community teams and neighborhoods.

Putting It All Together:
Families for Kids

The neighborhood is called Brooklyn Heights. It is in North Carolina. It is in fact a long way from Brooklyn. But the neighborhood is poor and struggling. It has big city problems in a rural small-town atmosphere. But it also has a lot of strong, caring citizens.

It was a late Saturday afternoon. Several individuals in the small, compact trailer court had called a meeting. Almost all the residents were there. People had pulled together cinderblocks to sit on. They placed them in a circle. They faced in toward one another. They began to talk. One after another, they shared stories about how their neighborhood had changed over the years. They were tired of being afraid. They wanted something different. They believed it could be different. They had come together to form a family support program. They had decided to band together to help one another. They invited the director of a nearby family support program to join them.

Families for Kids is a North Carolina child welfare reform initiative launched in the mid 1990s by the W. K. Kellogg Foundation. Its overall vision is greater permanence and safety for children. It employs a number of community and family interventions beginning with family support and prevention services and services directed to children entering and exiting from foster care. Participating communities seek to bring about a vision of greater permanence for families and children.

NESTED ACCOUNTABILITY

Central to North Carolina's overall approach is a philosophy of nested accountability and heightened responsibility for self-governance. The state has moved to replace top-down bureaucracy with increased local control beginning with the families themselves. North Carolina's nested accountability structure includes family support prevention services such as parent education, family group conferencing for those experiencing problems, community

assessment teams for those at risk of entering the child welfare system, and community self-evaluation teams to keep track of how
the community's overall approach is working. The capstone of
this nested accountability structure are voluntary local governance
groups facilitating the work of community partners and
eliminating unnecessary red tape and barriers as they are discovered. The local governance bodies are made up of a cross-
section of the community, its systems and its citizens.

Learning and
accountability
are self-regulating
and self-organizing
processes.

What is common to each level of this nested structure is
the location of learning and shared accountability squarely
with the community and its families. What is also common to
this structure is the placement of self-governance—responsibility
for self and service to others—squarely with the community and
its families. It is a community- and family-centered approach to
the support and care of children. Program staff, administrators,
neighbors, and representatives from the religious, business, and
civic communities are stewards to a process of shared learning and
accountability.

CHAPTER 9

Identifying Our Capacity for Shared Ownership and Governance

COMMUNITY VOICES As the individuals in the hall began to stand and move toward the exit, the director of the Cleveland County Department of Social Services turned to me and said, "Remember, this is not a democracy." I had just finished talking with a large gathering of employees in a public social services agency. Under the director's leadership, the agency had agreed to participate in an assessment of its organization. All the staff, nearly two hundred individuals from management to line staff, were being asked a series of questions through an online Internet assessment. They were being asked to identify both what their actual behavior was in a number of areas such as leadership, information management, and finances and what they would prefer it to be in those same areas. The slant of the assessment was clear. How open was the system now and how open would they prefer it to be? I asked them a hypothetical question on opportunities for leadership: "How many of you are leaders in your own homes?" A majority of hands shot up. I then asked them, "How many of you are leaders in your organization?" Only a few hands went up.

The statement "remember, this is not a democracy" has stayed with me. The director demonstrated remarkable courage in engaging in an open and reflective examination of the organization. Unmistakably however, she was ambivalent about doing so. Many of us share a similar ambivalence. All of us will have to summon our courage if we are to move from knowledge to action. Self-governance and democracy require courage. The director had courage. She had supported partnerships between the community and the social services agency—efforts in the areas of welfare, child welfare, and child support. She formed teams in the agency to participate in those partnerships. Now she felt the time was right to poll her staff on whether they were "walking the talk" of greater openness and partnership in the agency. It all made her nervous. She was not sure where it would lead, but she decided to trust the process. She called for a vote. While worrying about whether or not it could become more democratic, she in fact did move to democratize the organization further. After the vote, she supported the staff's call for greater openness. She listened. She followed through.

The Challenge of Self-Governance

All around the world, in both the private sector and in government, bureaucracies are opening up. The pressure to shift governance from the top of social institutions and organizations toward greater local and individual decision making and accountability is clear. The shift involves democratizing social institutions for those who work in them. It is also about reconnecting social institutions with their publics, their communities, and their families. In part, it is also about tempering our preoccupation with narrow individual and political self-interests in favor of greater responsibility for ourselves and service to others.

Shared ownership and accountability begins with personal responsibility.

Social institutions are in the process of rethinking and redesigning their governance structures—how we make decisions and behave. Senge et al. (1999) observed that the challenge to governance involves answering this question: "How will we balance the shift to greater local and personal decision making with a simultaneously increasing demand for interdependence at all levels?" In this dilemma is the timeless challenge to any democracy. How do we balance the interests of self—the I of individualism and special interest—with the collective we of family, community, and government? How do we balance our individual needs for self-control and self-determination with a growing acknowledgment of our interdependence?

Taking Responsibility for Self and Service to Others

The answer lies in you and me. It lies in people like us all over the country. In thinking about our troubles, Robert Greenleaf placed his finger squarely on our dilemma (Frick and Spears 1996). Greenleaf was an ardent advocate of leadership as stewardship. Stewards bring out the good in people. The troubles of the world, he said, are not so much the product of bad people as of the fact that good people—that means most of us—do not do better. Most people are trying to do the right thing, but something keeps getting in their way. Part of the answer to doing better lies in gathering the best knowledge and practices known to us. We can do that. We can build structures and processes that share learning and accountability. By doing this, we lay the foundation for ethical and effective personal and collective action.

Once we have informed ourselves and taken responsibility for our personal and collective learning and knowledge, what keeps us from acting on that knowledge? What keeps us from doing what we know is right? The answer lies is in our mind. It lies in how we go about trying to create a better world. To close the gap between knowing and doing, our first task is to reflect on how we traditionally think about doing—how we manage the process of change. Traditionally, we seek to control the process of change from the outside. This approach does not work well with complex social problems.

To balance society's overreliance on external authority and control, we must address a second important task: To articulate a set of principles that acknowledges our personal and collective capacities and gifts for steering the process of change. These principles support our role as stewards of our person, family, organization, and community. They support an approach to leadership and decision making by which we lightly steer, polish, and liberate both our capacity and the capacity of others for self-governance.

Barriers to Self-Governance

Before we explore the principles of stewardship and governance, it is useful to examine barriers to the exercise of those principles. When people return home from a community dialogue, they find it difficult to turn new knowledge into new behaviors. Knowledge alone, reclaiming our learning and accountability, does not guarantee changes in behavior. Even after embracing a philosophy of shared learning and accountability, it is as if we await permission from someone to act on what we know.

There are barriers to acting in accord with what we know. Chief among them is a powerful tendency to externalize our governance and our control to others. A distrust of those for whom we are a trustee—the community—and a narrow notion of self-interest are also barriers. We are often blinded by our short-term self-interest. We have a hard time envisioning long-term collective interests. The four serious barriers to shared ownership and governance for our social institutions are:

- Externalized governance

- Distrust of community

- Narrow self-interest

- Collective special interests

Peter Haus is the principal of an elementary school in a lower middle-class community of a midwestern city. His story is illustrative of those barriers. A community group approached Peter after a dialogue on education, asking whether he would be willing to make space available in his school for an after-school program for latchkey children. Peter doesn't see himself as having the power to make such a decision. Worried that the superintendent of the district would not be sympathetic to greater school and community involvement, Haus is reluctant to ask permission. He is not sure that he has the authority to develop a school-community partnership, and he is not all that sure he wants to get more involved with the community or how it will affect his job as principal. Nor is he sure that the teachers' union will support such a move.

Traditional approaches to leadership and responsibility in education and elsewhere are marked by a reluctance to redistribute power and authority within their own systems. They are also uncomfortable with sharing resources and power with other institutions and citizens in their community. It is a zero-sum world. Notions of personal, professional, and institutional interests are narrowly drawn and competitive. Paradoxically, Peter's approach undermines both his power and the power and influence of the professionals within the educational community. With time, the educational establishment becomes isolated and cut off from community support and resources. With time, it becomes less responsive to students and families. In turn it comes to feel unsupported and unrespected. Eventually it defeats its own best efforts to support families and serve the public.

Shared Ownership and Accountability

To promote shared ownership and accountability, we would do well to follow these four principles:

- Self-governance begins with taking responsibility.

- Place your trust in one another and the community.

- Model collaborative self-interest by both giving and receiving.

- Practice stewardship through service to others.

Kathryn Cramer's story illustrates these principles. The director of SMART Start, an early-childhood intervention program, Kathryn Cramer was at her desk at the family resource center late on a Saturday afternoon, trying to finish up her year-end reports to the state. There had been no time to do them during the week. There never was. She hated being away from her family on the weekend. She heard a hello from the hallway. A couple of neighborhood parents peered in the door. They knew she was doing the "dreaded reports."

An hour and a half later they reappeared. The two parents had multiplied into a small band. They had brought Kathryn a fried chicken dinner, complete with greens and homemade rolls. They also had brought an array of cleaning supplies. They placed the dinner on a table near her and gave her a hug. They dispersed throughout the center, cleaning it from top to bottom. Tomorrow after church services they were having a neighborhood luncheon at the center.

On a weekend in a family resource center, a community expressed itself. Individuals from different walks of life and with different roles in the neighborhood both withdrew something for themselves from the center and returned it in kind. They served one another in an atmosphere of familiarity, respect, and trust. They entered through different doors, with different needs and gifts, and created a community. The parents and the director were united by a desire to make life better for themselves, their families, and their community. They demonstrated responsibility for their part. They trusted one another. They gave as well as received. They served one another, united in a sense of moral commitment and common purpose. They demonstrated a sense of ownership for their behavior and their institution—the family resource center.

SELF-GOVERNANCE BEGINS WITH PERSONAL RESPONSIBILITY

Expressed in words, the challenge seems to be an oxymoron: *increased local and personal responsibility and greater collective interdependence.* In fact, the challenge of self-governance presents us with a paradox. For a couple of reasons, increased personal responsibility and authority for our behaviors and outcomes leads to both greater community and family and personal integration. First, it acknowledges that, at its most fundamental level, all conduct is individual. The authority to make decisions combined with a sense of moral commitment and ownership of results for ourselves, our families, and our organizations and communities is self-governance. Our ability to steer and control our own behavior is an expression of empowerment. In turn, when we improve our individual behavior and our personal standard of leadership, the behavior and standard of leadership of others around us improve.

A SEAMLESS WEB

Self-governance begins with the self and extends to others in a seamless web of service. Paradoxically, strength comes, not from our power over others, but rather from our power over ourselves and our willingness to honor and support each person's right to manage his or her own life. The true power we experience in relationships with others is not ours. It is earned and entrusted to us through a process of mutual support and respect. Power is a tremendous responsibility. It is to be used, whether as a spouse, parent, teacher, or community leader, to benefit those whose trustees we are (Nair 1997). We earn and retain power through service to others. We destroy that power and undermine our common purposes when we seek to control rather than to serve. Power earned through service integrates; power exercised through control isolates.

SELF-INTEREST RIGHTLY UNDERSTOOD

Tocqueville (1990) referred to our notion of self-governance as self-interest rightly understood. Individuals who assume responsibility for achieving their own purposes soon realize that most purposes cannot be reached by dint of individual effort alone. We hold many of our individual purposes—strong families, healthy and educated children—in common with diverse citizens throughout the community.

Shared ownership and accountability is modeled through the collaborative giving and receiving of support.

Securing individual and common purposes requires teamwork and collaboration. This recognition leads individuals to reach out to others to achieve through partnership what they cannot achieve alone. Self-governance contributes to collaborative partnerships and collective efficacy. At the core of each of us, at the center of self-governance, is a web of cooperative relationships (Senge and Kofman 1993).

Tips for Effective Self-Governance

The greatest mistake of self-governance dialogues and other attempts to foster civic involvement is to invite involvement and then exclude people from shared ownership and participation in decision making. Being informed, listening to diverse perspectives, and being open to their influence provides a foundation for leadership and action. Self-governance and stewardship provide others with the opportunity and responsibility to share the ownership of a problem, take possession of a situation, and contribute to a common vision. The principles of self-governance mark a shift from directing others to taking responsibility for oneself. As Greenleaf observed, stewardship both permits and invites others to step forward (Frick and Spears 1996). The price of that involvement must not be taken too lightly. Each of us, as stewards and leaders, must both facilitate the gifts and contributions of others and be open to their influence along the way. In doing this, we must trust in the goodness of people. We must believe that, if the means are right—participatory decision-making and shared responsibility—the ends will be right, the results better for communities and families. The principles and beliefs associated with self-governance can provide us with a guide as we move from understanding to action.

Shared ownership and accountability is fostered by holding ourselves responsible and placing our trust in each other and the community.

LINK MEANS AND ENDS—THE FUTURE IS NOW

One of the best ways for stewards and leaders to foster and maintain momentum is to treat the future as now. Just as we tend to break up and isolate social programs, communities, and individuals, we also treat means and ends, the present and the future, as if they were separate. They are not. The future is made by the means we employ in the present. If social institutions are to engage community and family, they must model community and support for family within the institution. If schools are to teach students to think and learn independently, they must model independence, learning, and creativity in the management of schools.

When the Cleveland County Department of Social Services assessed its own behavior and values, it found, across positions and program areas, that people wanted a more open, trusting community. The department was willing to engage and work on that common vision. It saw the connection between modeling community and family within the organization and its own efforts to engage communities and families through its work.

In the Higley Elementary School District in Phoenix, Arizona, charter schools and educational innovation have mushroomed. The Learning Institute, for example, is a small Phoenix school that features computer-assisted learning for at-risk students. Each student spends most of the day following an individualized program that reflects his or her unique interests and skills. Peer pressure and competition are minimized. There is little expectation that all the students should be at the same place. Adults circulate, ready to help when a student becomes stuck, bored, or in need of a change. By linking means and ends—individualized self-management, creativity, and learning—the future is being made by the means we use today.

FOSTER OWNERSHIP OF INSTITUTIONS AND DECISIONS

Who owns this place? In the case of a neighborhood resource center, a school, or a social services agency, the answer should be the community and its families. DePree (1989) observed that a sense of ownership "lends a rightness and permanence" to the relationship of each of us to our families and our social institutions. It heightens our sense of belonging and concern for one another. It demands an accountability and literacy for our families and community.

The parents in the SMART Start early intervention program and the Learning Institute feel a sense of ownership for their neighborhood resource center and community school. When you demonstrate ownership for what is happening to your family, your neighborhood center, and your school, you are more accountable for both personal and collective performance. You cannot walk away from problems. Ownership demands maturity from us all (DePree 1989).

BUILD DECISION MAKING AND PARTICIPATION FROM THE GROUND UP

When leaders create opportunities for citizens to participate in their social institutions and neighborhoods, they model stewardship and responsibility. Stewards of social institutions provide citizens with the appropriate services and tools to be responsive and accountable.

Stewardship is modeled through shared ownership and accountability

The city of Jacksonville, Florida, works hand in hand with its neighborhoods to engage government and community institutions in its Neighborhood Services Division. It is the "people's division." The city brings government closer to the average citizen through outreach programs, monthly citizen planning committees in every district, and matching neighborhood grants for innovative services. It also holds an annual Neighborhood Summit. It provides quick responses to the concerns of its citizens.

FOSTER MULTIPLE CENTERS OF POWER AND DECISION MAKING

Self-governance is supported when multiple centers of power exist in the community. Tocqueville (1990) and modern-day commentators such as McKnight (1995) have observed that the strength of American democracy rests on independent citizens and independent citizen associations. The dispersal of power, rather than its concentration, guarantees a free and democratic people.

Nonprofit institutions as well as government are experiencing heightened demands for accountability and economies of scale. Many good institutions and programs risk going under if they cannot demonstrate both accountability and economies of scale. Collaborative strategies to strengthen nonprofit institutions offer the best hope of preserving and even multiplying worthwhile programs. The nonprofit community is beginning to cut costs and share administrative overhead through collaborative strategies with former competitors (Bennett 1999). The North Carolina Center for Nonprofits opened in 1991 to assist other nonprofits in the state in the areas of management, finance, and technology. In Delaware, the DuPont Corporation provides both a space and a forum for collaboration. It donated a seventeen-story office building to house fifty nonprofit agencies.

In Jacksonville, Florida, a Human Service Council created in 1982 has taken on new life as human services turn to cooperative strategies for learning and adaptation. Partners include United Way, the state Department of Families and Children, the City of Jacksonville, the Chamber of Commerce, the Department of Juvenile Justice, and the Duval County School Board. They meet monthly to coordinate efforts and maximize resources and performance.

PROVIDE TRAINING AND CAPACITY BUILDING FOR STEWARDS

Stewardship of self-governing institutions requires that we strengthen our relationships with one another through ongoing communication and dialogue. Information must be shared openly, freely, and accurately among all partners. Communication and dialogue provide avenues for sharing best practices and feedback on how we are doing individually and collectively. This is how we support stewards of self-governance. This is also how we stay in touch and pass on our values and beliefs.

The Center for Servant Leadership in Indianapolis, Indiana, provides training on stewardship. The center was founded to honor and pass on the ideas and beliefs of Robert W. Greenleaf, an ardent advocate of leadership as stewardship. The Jordan Institute for Families in collaboration with the North Carolina Division of Social Services provides ongoing training and capacity building to support its emerging self-governing child welfare community. Leaders and managers are trained in open-system management

through a Leadership Roundtable Series. In open monthly meetings, training and dialogue opportunities are provided for community assessment and self-evaluation team coordinators.
Interdisciplinary line workers and family members are trained in
strength-based and family-centered practice.

SUPPORT COMMUNITY PARTNERSHIPS

Self-governance holds that everyone has the right and responsibility to influence and understand the results of decisions that affect
their families and communities. Our capacity for self-governance
grows out of our experience with shared ownership and governance. The Family Resource Coalition of America (FRCA) provides technical assistance and training to family support programs
and resource centers around the country. One of its most popular
and requested pieces of technical assistance is an exercise called
Making Room at the Table, in which FRCA provides tips and techniques for bringing everyone to the table to share through dialogue
in a participatory decision-making process. It is a process that
builds the capacity of families to govern themselves. It supports
parent leadership. It honors diversity and fosters respect for one
another, hallmarks of healthy communities and families.

In Hampton, Virginia, community leaders and activists reflect
these and other principles in an initiative launched in 1992 called
the Healthy Families Partnership. Through parent education,
home visiting programs, a teen pregnancy prevention program,
and accessible information in public library resource centers, the
community marshals its considerable talents and expertise. It is a
partnership whose goal is "to ensure that every child in Hampton
is born healthy and ready to learn."

RECONNECT SOCIAL INSTITUTIONS
TO THEIR PUBLICS

Citizens are reconnected to their public and private social institutions through self-governing structures and practices. People

breathe life back into the concept of citizenship. They reinvigorate and reclaim their democratic social institutions. Stewards of self-governance play an important role in supporting the principles and practices of participatory democracy. They help rebuild the capacity of social institutions to serve families and communities. In Hampton, Virginia, for example, a Neighborhood College holds an intensive four-month course for community leaders in the art of citizenship. The leaders develop an understanding of how city government works. Skills are refined for building partnerships and understanding between citizens and government.

Through these and other efforts like them, federal, state, and local governments are in the process of transforming themselves. An ethic of collaboration is developing and special interests are willing to work for the common good. Steven Kelman of Harvard University refers to this development as the emergence of a new "public spirit." It is public spirit that reconnects individuals to one another, to their neighborhoods, and to their social institutions. It is the essence of a participatory democracy.

Putting It All Together:
The Maureen Joy Charter School

Maureen Joy just sort of appeared. A small group of parents, current and former educators, and community activists were meeting in Cynthia Reade's office at Duke University. They were discussing starting a charter school in the Bragtown community. Joy heard that they were meeting and she wondered how she could help. Cynthia was sure Joy would not come back to the next meeting, but she did. A slight but enthusiastic woman, Maureen Joy was energetic beyond her years. She hung with the group as it took shape and began the daunting task of founding a charter elementary school. It was to be a school not just for any children. It was to be a school for children with special needs, children who fell between the cracks.

LEADERSHIP AND COMMUNITY

The school's theme is leadership and community. The school's mission is to unite a community of parents, educators, and others in supporting students to become confident, active learners and involved citizens. By creating positive, individualized instruction, the school is committed to building an educational community that emphasizes academic achievement, leadership, and community life.

The small voluntary band of citizens that formed the school's founding board is fiercely committed to keeping the light of learning lit in children. Without money for either buildings or transportation, the founders committed their own resources and those of other citizens to purchase trailers to house the first classes and two buses to transport the children. It took every bit of leadership in the group and an unbending sense of community to be ready for the opening school bell.

These citizens model responsibility and stewardship. They create opportunities for leadership. They instill a sense of community within the school. Children are provided opportunities to both learn and lead by sharing their learning and talents with other children. Parents contribute their time and talents to the school. They participate in their children's education. If parents cannot be there for parent–teacher conferences, the teacher goes to the parents' home. Students, parents, and teachers share ownership in both their school and the learning process. Nobody is asked to do anything that the person who is making the request would be unwilling to do him or herself. They are there for one another.

PASSION AND SPIRIT

When the school bell rang that first fall, a new charter school, ready or not, was launched. If anyone could keep a group's spirit up, passion engaged, and the candle of learning lit, it was Maureen Joy. She found the light in everyone and everything. She had passion. She had spirit. It helped carry them through the first year.

That passion crystallized itself several days before classes commenced. The finishing touches were put on the school grounds. The hot sweaty parents leaned on their rakes and shovels as they spread a tall mound of mulch in borders around the trailers. Joy reached down into the mulch. She had unexpectedly unearthed a flower. She held it up and exclaimed at her good fortune. She beamed. As everyone stood there and shared in the moment, a late afternoon rain began to fall. And wouldn't you know it, Joy turned her face to the sky. She embraced the rain as she had the flower, the children, the parents, the teachers, and the community.

A SMALL BAND OF CITIZENS

The price of innovation and institution building is not cheap. The first year was difficult. There were plenty of ups and downs. Everything was a challenge—the students, the parents, the community, and always, the finances. Only one of the four original teachers signed up to return the second year. But the board stayed the course, and so did Joy. New teachers were hired. Another grade was added. Students and parents came back. Joy was to become principal of the school. But just as school was to start, she passed away. Just as unexpectedly as she had appeared to help launch the new school, she disappeared.

Cynthia Reade left her job at Duke University. She and two other board members agreed to share the responsibilities of principal for the second year. The school bell rang and the second school year was underway. When the board met to discuss naming the school, the answer became obvious. It would be called the Maureen Joy Charter School. She typified responsibility balanced by humility, she displayed a commitment to serve others, and she exemplified an openness and joy in learning and living in the present.

CHAPTER 10

Creating a Culture of Self-Governance

COMMUNITY VOICES Less than a week after Hurricane Fran had torn through our neighborhood, I first met the neighbor who lived on the small hill behind us. Looking out the window from our living room, I saw him working diligently trying to clear away fallen trees and limbs with a small electric chain saw. Before the trees came down, I had never even noticed he was there. I introduced myself. We cleared away some of the limbs together. We found that we had young children near in age. He, his wife, and children had been in their home for nearly two years but our paths had never crossed. It was as if the trees had blocked what was later to become a meaningful relationship.

In the months and now several years since the storm, we have spent many pleasant times together. Our children and the children of another neighbor to the east of us came and played in one another's homes. We watched, encouraged, and disciplined one another's children. We had dinners together. We exchanged tips on parenting and much more. We supported one another. And we had fun. We also shared some difficult times. Our friend's father-in-law died quickly of cancer. And our friend's marriage was in trouble. We spent many hours talking on long walks. Good people were going through a difficult, wrenching time. Eventually, he moved out and away. Our relationship with his wife and children continues. We were saddened over our lost relationship with him.

And it all started when a few trees were toppled in a storm and we were able to see each other for the first time. When the trees came down, the distance between us collapsed. And through conversation and common interests, a relationship blossomed that has changed each of us forever.

After the Hurricane, The Challenge of Culture

Whether through a natural disaster such as a hurricane, social shifts such as welfare and school reform, or personal losses such as a divorce or an unexpected death, traditional relationships and values are challenged. Sometimes they are transformed. These events and changes challenge the way we normally do things. Community dialogues represent similar, although not as intense, challenges to the way in which we normally do things. They challenge our expectations of one another and ourselves. Efforts to sustain the momentum for change often run counter to our most deeply held values and assumptions. They often run into a wall of both personal and collective resistance called culture.

Senge et. al. (1999) refer to culture as a sixth sense. It shapes the choices that individuals and organizations see or do not see as they seek to adapt to internal and external challenges and survive over time. The intangible of culture gives rise to tangible structures, processes, and behaviors. The ways in which we structure our relationships and behaviors within families, between families, and within and between organizations are no more and no less than crystallized beliefs and values. They are our culture.

When the trees came down between my family and my neighbors, an opportunity to connect and build a greater sense of community presented itself. We took advantage of it. As a result, we have experienced both the benefits and greater demands of an interdependence that we call friendship and community. When the bureaucratic walls come down between programs and citizens, all parties involved experience both the benefits and demands of interdependence. The creation of interdisciplinary and multiagency teams in the public social services enhances decision making but demands greater information sharing and shared control. Placing parents and citizens at the center of decision making requires both greater trust on everyone's part and shared responsibility.

Self-governing cultures recognize and value interdependence.

Sustaining the momentum for increased self-governance calls for a shift in culture. It requires a shift in traditional values and assumptions about leadership, accountability, relationships, information, and communication. It requires that we change the structures we have erected to support these beliefs. It requires, as Tocqueville (1990) observed, that we honor and respect the "habits of the heart" our yearning and need for a greater sense of interdependence in both family and community.

Habits of the Mind, Overcoming a Culture of Separation

Tocqueville feared the growth of a narrow individualism in this country. In it he foresaw, more than a hundred years ago, an emerging threat to our freedom and well-being. In this individualism, people imagine that they personally hold their entire destiny in their hands. As a result they isolate themselves from their fellow citizens. They eventually forget their elders and neglect their descendants—

Self-governing cultures value dialogue.

their children. The social capital, the bonds and relationships, within families and between families and community, is weakened.

As a culture, whether we are talking about parents who do not know what their children are doing under the same roof or human services fragmented by categorical thinking and careerism, we are increasingly shut up in the solitude of our own worlds. Robert Bellah, the author of *Habits of the Heart,* referred to it as a "culture of separation." It is a culture in which citizens operate out of mental images and habits that undermine their solidarity with one another.

As early as 1611, the English poet John Donne captured what is increasingly a modern refrain, "Tis all in peeces, all cohaerence gone." When citizens return from a community self-governance dialogue, they return to a culture of separation and isolation. They return to a culture characterized by pieces and fragments. They return to a culture where there is little synergy or coherence in their work, family, or community. The network of relationships that is necessary if we are to get things done—the social capital—is depleted.

Our traditional values and beliefs make it difficult to imagine, let alone construct, a more coherent and holistic world. Careers and self-interest override and fragment our sense of common purpose. Independence is valued to the point of isolation. Relationships are undermined by competitive assumptions that frame conversations and interactions in win-lose terms. People approach one another and the prospect of change with wariness and a distrust of one another's motives. Communication is used to assert control over others and promote self-interest. It is less often employed for reflection and self-control or for listening and trying to understand others.

A short story illustrates our culture of separation. The conference was underway. The speaker had written extensively on family and community; she had heard his name many times before. When he finished the lecture, she went up to the lectern to speak with him. Finally, she caught his attention. She introduced herself. She complemented him on his presentation. It meant a lot to her, she said. He thanked her. He asked her what she did for a living. She said she was a full-time parent. It was as if she had said something terrible. Immediately his eyes and attention slipped away. He looked right through her as if searching for a more worthy audience. Her face felt hot. It stung. It was as if she had been slapped. What she hoped was understanding and connection was neither. She felt separation and distance.

Habits of the Heart, Creating a Culture of Self-Governance

Self-governance dialogues are forums for discussions and communication regarding our core values and morality. They are discussions of our culture. They ask us to examine and reflect on our "habits of the heart." Such dialogues take place in communities— organizations, churches, and community centers. They also occur at the dinner table among family members.

Self-governance dialogues tap into the spirit of the heart as well as the mind. They tap into love and our desire to belong and to make a difference in someone's life. These aspirations are present in each one of us. By employing the language of the heart—purpose, dreams, and potential, and not of problems or blame—dialogues lead to uncovering values that unite us as family and community. Dialogues are discussions of value and morality (Etzioni 1996) that replenish the spirit. They create a family's and a community's social capital.

Self-governing cultures recognize people as being driven by common purposes and aspirations

Abraham Maslow, the father of humanistic psychology (1999), held that each of us is born with an innate drive for self-actualization. The innate drive is accompanied by a need to experience higher values such as beauty, peace, and justice. The aspiration to higher values and self-actualization mirrors and complements the values and beliefs that accompany our drive to be self-governing—to control our private and collective selves. Self-governance and self-actualization are two halves of a complementary whole. We each possess a potential for self-actualization and self-governance. The question is not why some people, organizations, and communities govern themselves but rather why more are not self-governing. They are not self-governing because their values and beliefs rest on fear, control and compliance and their institutions and behaviors would need to be redesigned around values and beliefs that support the potential for self-governance.

Values and beliefs that support and honor our capacity for self-governance include purpose, trust, interdependence, cooperation, and dialogue. These values and beliefs assume that each of us is driven by a belief in a higher purpose, a capacity for trustworthiness, a willingness to acknowledge our interdependence, a belief in change and growth through cooperation, and an ability to use dialogue to become more self-governing and self-actualizing.

The values and beliefs that underlie self-governing communities and families may be expressed in these words:

• People are driven by purpose and aspiration.

• People are trustworthy.

- People recognize and value interdependence.

- People recognize and value cooperation.

- People value dialogue.

PEOPLE ARE DRIVEN BY PURPOSE AND ASPIRATION

In Colorado Springs, Colorado, David Berns and Barbara Drake
(1999) are stewards for a Department of Human Services that
serves El Paso County. In their work they model the values and
beliefs of self-governance, assuming that people, irrespective of
their position in the organization or community, are motivated by
a common sense of a purpose and a personal aspiration to make a
positive difference in the lives of their families and communities.
Such beliefs are a foundation on which families become self-
governing and self-actualizing.

These values and beliefs are reflected in the mission of the
department, which is to employ human services as tools to
"strengthen families, assure safety, promote self-sufficiency, elimi-
nate poverty, and improve the quality of life in our community."
The department assumes that the individuals and families for
which it is steward seek to strengthen themselves, ensure the safety
of those in their care, and become economically and socially self-
sufficient. They may struggle and falter, but on the whole they are
motivated by similar beliefs and values.

PEOPLE ARE TRUSTWORTHY

In working with the community and those families and children in
its care, the department assumes that people are fundamentally
trustworthy. It trusts that people are well intentioned. It trusts that
people seek responsibility and accountability. It trusts that people
seek meaning in their personal and work lives. It trusts that people
want to learn and can change. In assuming the best in people, the
department approaches each individual, not for what he or she is
not, but for what he or she aspires to be. Information is shared and
participation in decision making is encouraged within a context of

accountability. There are incentives and consequences for violating the spirit of trust and openness with families, staff, and community collaborators. The department finds that, more often than not, people step up to the expectations and challenges.

PEOPLE RECOGNIZE AND VALUE INTERDEPENDENCE

El Paso County's approach to human services recognizes and supports interdependence. Previously separate programs such as child welfare, Temporary Assistance to Needy Families (TANF), child support, Medicaid, child care, food stamps, and so on, are restructured into a unified system that supports a common mission. For example, TANF savings that have accompanied the decline in the welfare rolls are being used to support early intervention and prevention services. Early intervention programs in the areas of fathering, prevention of teen pregnancy, work preparation, and kinship care address the root causes of poverty and family disruption. In the long run, the approach pays handsome dividends to the entire community in more productive and healthy citizens.

PEOPLE RECOGNIZE AND VALUE COOPERATION

The El Paso Department of Human Services fosters cooperation both within the department and between the department and the larger community that it serves. By knocking down the walls between categorical programs, the department creates opportunities for collaboration within the agency. By subcontracting with a range of nonprofit service providers in the community, the department builds a collaborative safety net for the community's families and children.

The department believes that building relationships on a cooperative, win-win basis makes use of previously untapped resources for the community's families and children. It is a belief that assumes that cooperative, respectful relationships generate new energy and resources for people. It is a belief in a world of abundance and possibility.

PEOPLE VALUE DIALOGUE

The El Paso Department of Human Services assumes that people are willing to enter into a dialogue for change. It assumes that people do not dislike change so much as being changed. Whether in family-centered practice, support programs for grandparents raising grandchildren, or its program for fathers, the department practices the art of respectful dialogue. It is a practice that promotes greater responsibility for self and service to others. It is a practice that assumes that there are several sides to the same story and that solutions to our problems lie somewhere in the middle. Dialogue, because it encourages listening and the creation of shared meaning, creates an opportunity for staff, community collaborators, and families alike to shape change.

SELF-GOVERNANCE, CULTURE, AND SOCIAL CAPITAL

Families and communities are wealthy when they can draw on a network of relationships to get things done, solve problems, and achieve dreams. Social capital is the measure of that wealth. It is a measure of the give and take in relationships. It is a measure of the fabric and richness of family and community networks. It is a measure of the values and beliefs that hold these relationships together.

At the family level, nuclear and extended family networks are a source of mentoring and of moral, spiritual, social, and economic support. The family is the safety net and social and economic springboard of first resort. In families rich in social capital, the finely stitched and dense network of relationships helps adults and children alike get ahead. In families in which the fabric of relationships is threadbare, the members may barely get by or may be held back.

At the community level, social capital is generated through participation in civic and social institutions such as the Young Men's Christian Association (YMCA), soccer leagues, voluntary associations, church groups, schools, and health and human services organizations. Social capital is measured in a community's ability to bring diverse groups and perspectives to solve complex social problems. Children rich in family and community social capital receive a tremendous head start in life.

The culture and philosophy of self-governance, by fostering responsibility for one's own behavior and service to others, creates social capital for both families and communities. The abundance or absence of social capital is a reflection of both family and community culture and of the interlaced nature of family and community relationships. The core values of self-governance—purpose, trust, interdependence, cooperation, and dialogue—are the constituents of social capital. The values of a narrowly individualistic, competitive, isolated, and distrustful culture deplete a society's social capital and well being.

Creating a Culture of Self-Governance

To create a culture of self-governance and the social institutions and behaviors that accompany that culture, we must turn many of our traditional beliefs and assumptions on their heads. For many of us, that means changing our assumptions about human nature. We must, as Maslow observed (1999), stop selling people short. A culture of self-governance assumes that people by their nature are purpose driven, trustworthy, responsible, fair, and embrace learning. Traditional social institutions and practices assume that people are primarily self-promoting, do only what is required, shirk responsibility, and resist learning. Self-governance assumes that it is the potential—not the problems and shortcomings—of people that is our most important asset. It is possible to create a culture of self-governance that taps into the potential of individuals to strengthen families. It is possible to rethink relationships and redesign social institutions to maximize the contributions of people. It is possible to maintain the momentum for social change.

Self-governing cultures recognize people as basically trustworthy.

ASSUME THE BEST: THE 98–2 RULE

The first tip for creating a culture of self-governance is to "assume the best about people." It is similar to taking a strength or asset perspective in working with families and communities. If we are to get the best from people—responsibility, creating, learning, and a willingness to change—we must assume that they are capable of the same.

I try to remember this tip in my work as associate director of the Jordan Institute for Families and as a father and husband by using what I call the 98–2 rule: In working with people, if something happens that leads you to imagine that someone is trying to undercut you, is not being fully honest or forthcoming, stop and consider the following. Ninety-eight percent of the time when a negative inference is drawn, the real problem is one of communication and understanding; often, something simple explains what is going on. For example, the Jordan Institute needed a letter from North Carolina's governor to move on a project in the area of family support. The director of the state Division of Social Services, Kevin FitzGerald, volunteered to help secure the letter. Weeks went by and nothing was happening. When I checked periodically, I found very busy people struggling to get a million things done. I did not find a lack of support or stonewalling. It was frustrating for all parties concerned, but it was not because they did not support what we were trying to do. Now 2 percent of time—sometimes only 1 percent of the time—someone *is* out to get you. Some people cannot be trusted. Some people do not want to learn. Some people *are* not responsible. But they are far and away the minority. The vast majority of people struggle to do the right thing. It always pays to assume the best, to check out your inferences, and to keep on cooperating.

IDENTIFY COMMON VALUES

A second tip is to identify the values that we have in common. Common values such as purpose—ensuring the safety and well-being of children—and operating from a base of trust, cooperation, and respect bring people together. Focusing on what we have in common, rather than on the differences that divide us, provides a foundation for learning and change.

In the McKnight neighborhood in Springfield, Massachusetts, citizens came together with the Family Support Program without Walls to reassert their values and reclaim their community. For years, citizens had witnessed the deterioration of their community, its institutions, economic base, and sense of civility and values. They watched as the youth of their community lost their respect for social institutions and for adults. They watched a community lose its own sense of self-respect. By going door to door, citizens canvassed their neighbors and fellow citizens to identify those values they held in common. Elders, parents, teachers, community policemen, family support workers, and citizens from diverse walks of life identified values for reclaiming order and civility in their community. Chief among these values are a sense of trust, cooperation, and interdependence. The restatement of common values is a beacon for uniting people around a sense of hope and possibility.

Self-governing cultures recognize and value cooperation.

Whether we are talking about the McKnight neighborhood or countless neighborhoods like it, the popularity of William Bennett's *Book of Virtues,* or the growth of institutes and centers on civics and civility, we are witnessing a growing national reflection on our core values. Through this reflective process, we will find values we hold in common. They will provide that foundation for reshaping our culture and our social institutions.

IDENTIFY THE GAPS

The third tip is to identify the gaps between actual and preferred behavior. For example, although New York City's crime rate has dropped dramatically in recent years, the decline has, in many instances, been accompanied by a rise in complaints about rude and brutal police behavior. The assumption in policing has been that you trade some of your rights and civility for safety on the streets. It was assumed that crime could not be reduced without damaging police and community relations; it was assumed that there would be a trade-off; it was assumed that it could not be a win-win situation. In 1994, when community policing was instituted, police complaints rose 36 percent.

It does not have to be that way. It is possible to secure meaningful change while honoring and respecting those we are working with and for. In New York City, the South Bronx's Forty-second and Forty-fourth Precincts are a case in point. In 1995, roughly 165,000 people lived in those two precincts. Nearly two-thirds received welfare, and unemployment ranged between 14 and 17 percent. More than 95 percent of the people were African American or Hispanic; 70 percent of the police force was white. Despite the obvious challenges, both crime and police complaints have dropped in recent years. Captain Tom King, commander of the Forty-second Precinct, has demonstrated a commitment to deliver the whole package: "safer streets and people who respect us because we respect them. Why accept less?" Both King and Richard Romaine, the commander of the Forty-fourth Precinct, made it clear that repeated complaints would not be tolerated. Both men had the same goal—reducing citizen complaints while not letting up on crime fighting.

GO THE EXTRA MILE IN CLOSING THE GAPS

Identifying common values and the gaps between present and preferred values and behaviors sets the stage for taking action to close those gaps. It sets the stage for "being the change and behaving the values" we want to see in others. The tip here is that we ourselves must be willing to take the first step and sometimes go the extra mile in modeling the values and behaviors we hold important.

In the British "patch" approach to community-centered service delivery modeled in Cedar Rapids, Iowa, human services workers, rather than just waiting for citizens to come to them, stepped forward and went to the community. Human services staff are located in the community neighborhoods they serve rather than downtown or in some other distant office. For example, one of the probation officers on a human services team stepped forward to offer

Tae Kwon Do lessons in the gymnasium of a church where a patch office was located. It turned out to be the spark that made the patch project a big hit. Where families were reluctant to get involved initially with the neighborhood program, the personal and informal touch brought parents and children forward to participate, connect, and support one another.

FOCUS ON PARTICIPANTS; IGNORE THE LOOKY-LOOS

Dave Hickey at the University of Nevada at Las Vegas, in writing about art and democracy, divides the world into two kinds of people—the looky-loos and the participants. In *Essays on Art and Democracy,* he describes the looky-loos as those people who attend but do not participate. They do not embrace either the values or the essence of what you are trying to bring about. They look but they do not buy. Participants, however, fortified by values and beliefs that embrace the new and challenging, are willing to embrace the cause. They are willing to take part in efforts to open up the culture. They are willing to hang with you in both good and bad times.

Whether we are working with parents taking active roles in the lives of their children, engaging neighbors in a community development project, or unleashing the potential of employees in public institutions, we will always run across more than our fair share of looky-loos. At times, each of us is a looky-loo if the issue does not engage us or we do not have the time to take on another cause. The tip here is to start with the committed participants and move to expand their circle. It helps, as we do this, to remember the observation that is attributed to Margaret Mead: "Never doubt that a small group of thoughtful committed citizens can change the world. Indeed, it's the only thing that ever has."

HOLD OURSELVES ACCOUNTABLE

Jan Arnow does not go for the simplistic solutions. She does not believe that the events in Littleton, Colorado, Paducah, Kentucky, Springfield, Oregon, Pearl, Mississippi, Jonesboro, Arkansas, or

Conyers, Georgia, could have been prevented with categorical solutions such as gun and media control. They are easy targets, but the focus is misplaced. Arnow, the mother of three, holds that real solutions will come about only when every adult and youth accepts responsibility for the kind of climate and culture that contributes to youth violence. She formed a project called No More Violence to drive her point home. Through the project, she conducts a bus tour for adults in Louisville, Kentucky, pointing out the cracks in society where violent influences come into the lives of children. The tour includes video stores, arcades, toy stores, gun shops, movie theaters, and our own television sets—all of which convey messages of violence and permissiveness in our culture. The questions she poses to parents are, "Are you satisfied with what's going on with your kids?" and "What are you doing to take responsibility for the influences that come into your children's lives?" The message that she conveys to parents and the community is that given the environment that we have created through our culture, youth violence should not come as a surprise. The tip here is to hold ourselves personally accountable and lead by example. There are no scapegoats—each of us must take responsibility for what is going on in our homes, our neighborhoods, and the larger culture.

CELEBRATE OUR CULTURE

A last tip for creating a culture of self-governance is to celebrate our values and the process of building that culture. It is both important and acceptable to talk about the role of values in social institutions, communities, and families. Values and culture are the essence of what we are about as a society.

When the Department of Social Services in Cleveland County, North Carolina, assessed its organizational culture, trust was the value for which there was the biggest gap between actual and preferred behavior. An agencywide dialogue was convened to identify strategies for closing this and other gaps. A team was formed to oversee the implementation of the strategies to foster a greater sense of partnership among the agency, its staff, and the community. The team set to work on making the agency more family and community friendly. The waiting room was made more inviting, and an effort was undertaken to establish evening hours for parents who worked during the day.

The team also realized that if it were to be successful in partnering with the community out there, it needed to model a sense of community in here—within the agency. The starting point would be to stage the first-ever agency picnic for staff and their families. The team took responsibility for raising the money and planning the picnic, which created a free space in which staff were able to get to know one another as whole people with interests both inside and outside work. It was designed to help personalize and build a community culture within the organization. Personalizing relationships and creating space for community-building activities is an avenue for building greater trust within the agency.

It Begins at Home

Culture is like the air we breathe. It permeates every nook and cranny, every level of society. But there is a common agreement that our cultural hearth is found in the home. The hard work of building a culture of self-governance takes place in each of our homes. When do we begin? We must begin now. Many of the principles and values of self-governance are embedded in the personal challenges that we each face daily. The principles and process of self-governance as they apply to families and communities are captured in this book. In many ways they mirror Stephen Covey's work (1997) on the habits of effective families. We begin the work of self-governance and creating effective families with a clear vision of the end we have in mind—the destination we want for ourselves and our family. We start by taking personal responsibility for the journey. We begin by taking the first step. We continue by placing one foot in front of the other as we make the journey.

My son Alec was three and my daughter Alexis was seven when we sat down for our first family meeting at the dinner table. We gathered to talk about what kind of life we wanted for our family. We had decided to create a statement of what we wanted for our family and the rules and principles we would try to live by.

After some giggling and fidgeting, the statement of what we wanted for our family was framed in the words "to be happy and to help one another." As things settled down, we went around the circle, taking turns in identifying the rules we believe in and want to live by. Alexis was the scribe. The following were the rules we came up with that Sunday evening as she wrote them down. She was the author of the first; Alec of the last.

What We Want—To Be Happy and to Help Each Another

RULES AND PRINCIPLES WE BELIEVE IN

- Be respectful of other people.

- Always be helpful and clean up after yourself.

- Listen when someone else is talking.

- Try to solve your problems yourself before asking for help.

- Do not say bad things behind people's back!

- Do not hurt other people.

- Do not yell in the house.

- Always tell the truth.

- Flush the toilet.

- Ask somebody if you can come in their room.

- Wash your hands before eating.

- Do not write on the walls.

The statement and rules and principles, were posted on the refrigerator door.

On Sunday evenings, with occasional lapses, we sit down as a family and go over the past week and plan for the upcoming week. We begin the conversation by having each person say something positive about another family member—to describe something that that person did to make another feel good. Each family member has an opportunity also to mention something he or she is not happy with—some interaction or behavior. As each person talks, the others listen. When one person is addressing another, they hold hands. The touch connects. It makes the conversation personal and safe. We conclude by identifying how each person will help around the home in the upcoming week.

Stephen Covey called it habit number three—putting first things first. Making the time for family and family meetings is essential if family is to be a priority. Oprah Winfrey also said it— if you can't make the time available, you do not value family. Each of us knows what we should do—doing it consistently is the challenge.

Putting It All Together

Putting it all together—easy to say, but hard to do. And yet when you start listening to people and really hear what they are saying, you begin to believe that we each want many of the same things. We want our personal and work lives to be less fragmented and more integrated. We want to be more trusting and cooperative with one another. We want a better fit between our core values and the values and behaviors of our family and social institutions. We want to feel connected, part of something greater than ourselves. We want to be part of something that nourishes and support our families and communities.

All across the country and even all around the world it is, as Kurt Lewin, the well-known systems theorist, observed, as if our environment and our souls are asking for something to be done.

We know something has gone wrong. We are beginning to heed a call to straighten it all out—to make it whole again. We are talking and listening to one another more. We are developing new and more respectful partnership between government and its citizens. We are beginning to see things more holistically. And as we begin to feel more integrated with our world, the more annoying we find and the less tolerant we are of the continuing fragmentation and isolation.

Maslow (1999) in thinking about the management of our social institutions and their relationship to each of us, saw his goal as "resacralizing" our institutions and our relationship with them. To resacralize our institutions, including our families and communities, we must make them worthy of veneration. The philosophy of self-governance does that. Rather than building our institutions and relationships with them around our fears of what we are not—our shortcomings and deficits—we must found them on a belief on what we aspire to be—responsible, creative, compassionate, loving, and ethical. Until we found our families, communities, and institutions on values and behaviors that we venerate, we cannot respect, love, nor trust ourselves or our institutions.

Predialogue Planning and Preparations

Self-governance dialogues bring out the intelligence and creativity that all communities and organizations possess. Participants experience the interdependence of their organizations and communities. Through dialogue, they

- Acknowledge that interdependence

- Create a vision of the future

- Identify the different paths for moving into this future

- Select the path they will use to create this future

Successful change involving the communities and organizations that serve families and children can and frequently does depend on small, seemingly inconsequential factors. Four of these factors must be carefully addressed in the planning:

1. The community must be fully represented at the self-evaluation event.

2. The role of the facilitators is that of stewards in a process of liberation and empowerment.

3. A pre-event performance assessment must be conducted.

4. There must be commitment to the process.

FULL REPRESENTATION OF THE COMMUNITY

Most strategic planning events include too many people from the service systems and too few people who are consumers or other key stakeholders. Planning is usually conducted by a group of service system representatives who develop expert plans for changing the behavior of others. It frequently does not adequately involve the governed or other key players. As a result, it often results in wrapping services around families and children, isolating them further from the community, and making their problems worse.

Effective self-governance dialogues involve representatives of all community institutions, associations, and citizens. The structure of community institutions and associations is built on voluntary consent and choice, whereas many traditional service institutions are built on production and control. Communities include many associations that, because of their interdependence and intimacy, possess a capacity to respond rapidly to the needs of citizens. Services are more likely to produce desired outcomes when they help form family ties to voluntary, small-scale, face-to-face community associations and institutions. So, self-governance events are most effective when between 25 and 40 percent of those in attendance represent citizens, community groups, and stakeholders outside the service system.

FACILITATORS AS STEWARDS

Self-governance dialogues and community and family service institutions are most effective when the facilitators and the representatives of the service system behave as stewards. Stewardship rests on the belief that others have the knowledge and answers within themselves. Facilitators of the self-governance dialogues and community service providers can set up a process and create an environment that permits participants to discover their own answers and take responsibility for them. This process and environment involves dialogue and collaborative partnerships. Stewardship encourages participants to talk about their doubts, limitations, hopes, and aspirations and it makes everyone part of a common dialogue. It recognizes that participants' ability to improve results for others depends on their willingness to work together to change themselves.

Successful collaborative partnerships in support of improved outcomes for families and children depend on the commitment by all participants to assume responsibility for defining the community's vision and its values and acting to support that vision. Collaborative partnerships succeed when all members are accountable for failures and successes and make a commitment to ongoing dialogue and learning. Facilitators make this happen by supporting ownership and choice and expecting responsibility and accountability at every level.

PRE-EVENT PERFORMANCE ASSESSMENTS

A key step in the self-governance process is the pre-event performance assessment. This stage-setting activity includes

- Assessing actual performance honestly and dispassionately

- Developing the agenda and activities associated with the event

- Establishing the roles and responsibilities of the host community and organization

Pre-event performance assessments are usually conducted in a one-day meeting several months before the self-governance dialogue. In this performance assessment, the community clarifies the outcomes for which it proposes to hold itself accountable and assembles much of the common database that will provide the community and its service organizations with an understanding of both current and future outcomes. This common database describes the strengths and needs of children and families and it describes the community's failures and successes in serving them over time.

The facilitators and the host organization review guidelines for identifying outcomes and pulling together the common database before the preliminary meeting. At this meeting, key representatives of the community, organizations, and consumer representatives prioritize desired outcomes and develop a common database. The outcomes and initial common database are written up for presentation during the self-governance dialogue.

This is also a good time to address the importance, role, and function of performance teams and partnerships in the ongoing process of change. Performance teams will be formed during the dialogue and consist of representatives from the community and organizations. These teams will

- Keep score on outcomes

- Collect, analyze, and present findings on outcomes

- Determine what works and what does not work

- Feed the information back into the self-governance process in a timely fashion

COMMITMENT TO THE PROCESS

Self-governance dialogues are most likely to succeed when the community and organization hosting the event are fully committed to the process. During the dialogue, the facilitators help participants find their own answers to persistent challenges. A community and organizational commitment to test these new answers depends on a willingness to renegotiate issues of power, control, and choice.

Facilitators cannot and should not presume to negotiate, summarize, or develop the results. Dialogue facilitators will not hand the host any answers at the end of the event. The community and host organization assume full responsibility and ownership for developing their own

- Common database

- Desired outcomes

- Vision

- Action plan

Setting Up the Dialogue: Logistics and Site

Successful dialogues depend on solid organization and attention to detail. In planning a self-governance dialogue, careful attention must be paid to:

- Invitations

- Facilitators

- The site

- Work groups

- Posting of shared group information

- Materials

- Amenities

AGENDA

The host organization reviews the agenda before the initial meeting and finalizes it during the initial meeting. The agenda appears here as figure 6.

FIGURE 6: **Self-Governance Process at a Glance**

DAY 1	DAY 2	DAY 3
Welcome	Look Back: Mapping "What Is"	Community Promises:
Building Community	Strategies	Commitment to Community
Icebreaker: The Golden Egg	Actions	Valentines
Introductions	Norms and Beliefs	
		Aligning Action with Future
A Self-Governance	Paradigm Shift: Creating a	Plans
Explaining the 3-day process	Bridge Between Current	Valentines Revisited
Explaining the Performance	and Future	
Model	Changing Mental Maps	Public Accountability for
View from Leadership	Shifting Mental Maps	Performance
		Contracts
Establishing a Common Reality:	Create the Future: Mapping	Homework
Identifying Performance Gaps	the Future	Scorecard
Telling our Stories	Strategies	
	Actions	
Owning Outcomes	Norms and Beliefs	
Present at the Creation		
100-Percent Responsibility		
Individual Leads to the		
Collective		

ROLES AND RESPONSIBILITIES OF THE HOST ORGANIZATION

The host organization's responsibilities include:

- Securing a qualified facilitator
- Participating in the pre-event meeting and performance assessment
- Setting a time and place for the event
- Working with others to identify participants
- Inviting participants to attend the event
- Acting as a host for the self-governance dialogue
- Participating in the postevent debriefing

The host's responsibilities for the logistics and site of the event are outlined in the concluding section of this appendix (see page 199). Remember that the self-governance dialogue will be most likely to succeed when between 25 and 40 percent of the participants are from outside the service provider arena.

WHOM TO INVITE

The participant list should include representatives from the following organizations:

- The host organization
- Funding sources
- Related organizations in the service system
- Family support services
- Respite and crisis care services
- Child welfare services
- Education services
- Juvenile justice services

- Other organizational stakeholders
- Schools
- Family service agencies
- Courts
- Child mental health
- Public health
- Private nonprofit agencies that serve families
- Citizens
- Consumers who are the direct beneficiaries of the primary host organization
- The community at large
- Churches
- Civic and neighborhood associations
- The business community
- The police
- Unions

INVITATIONS

The host sets a date and place for the self-governance dialogue. The invitations give sufficient notice so that participants can plan to attend.

FACILITATORS

The self-governance process is most effective when outside consultants act as facilitators. Because the experts on change and performance are the participants—consumers, citizens, human services providers, and others—the role of the facilitators is to support the process of self-managed dialogue, discovery, and change. For this reason, facilitators must be comfortable with large groups and understand their dynamics. They must be prepared to assist participants in uncovering values and beliefs behind current approaches to performance and in framing and articulating new strategies and beliefs for improved performance and outcomes. Facilitators must be comfortable with letting people struggle but capable of stopping the process if participants turn to unproductive conflict or avoidance.

SETTING UP THE SITE

Figure 7 provides a diagram of how individual tables and the room as a whole can be arranged for best results. Self-governance dialogues involve large numbers of people, from several dozen to several hundred. Planners should select a room big enough to accommodate large groups comfortably. A room that is forty by fifty feet can accommodate sixty-four people seated at eight tables in groups of eight. (Between eight and ten people at a table is generally ideal.) Round tables, rather than rectangular ones, encourage interaction among participants. Chairs should be comfortable, and the room should have adequate lighting and good climate control. Large rooms should be equipped with sound systems.

The room is set up in the shape of the performance diamond (see the following page) that is used to structure the performance dialogue. At the center of the room is a table where common data can be displayed. In one corner of the room there is a flip chart for posting current outcomes. In the opposite corner of the room there is another flip chart for posting future outcomes. On the left side, current performance strategies can be posted, either on the wall or on a portable screen or flip charts. Similarly, on the right side, performance strategies for the future can be posted. A registration table for participants should be placed either outside or out of the way near the entrance to the room.

MIX-AND-MATCH SELF-MANAGED WORK GROUPS

Figure 8 on page 202 shows the makeup of the work groups formed at the event. The tables indicate a mix of consumers,

FIGURE 7: **Setting Up the Site**

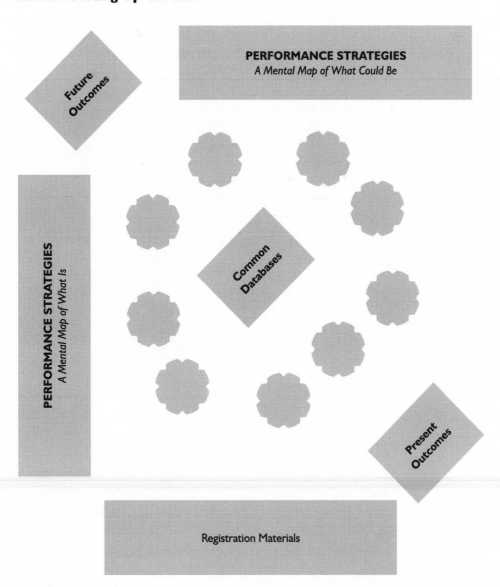

FIGURE 8: **Participants in Self-Managed Groups**

3 Resident x 8
2 Comity Stakeholder x 8
2 Agency Rep x 8
1 information system x 8
Spe

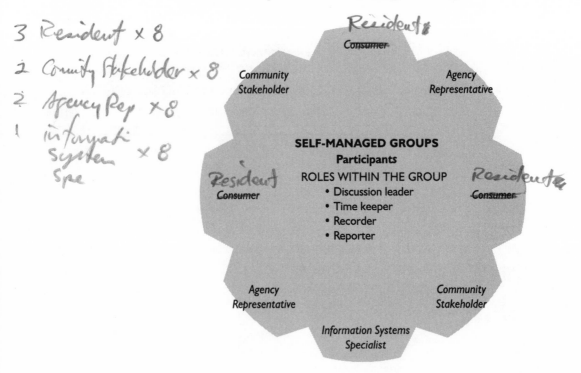

Resident
Consumer

Community
Stakeholder

Agency
Representative

SELF-MANAGED GROUPS
Participants
ROLES WITHIN THE GROUP
• Discussion leader
• Time keeper
• Recorder
• Reporter

Resident
Consumer

Resident
Consumer

Agency
Representative

Community
Stakeholder

Information Systems
Specialist

citizens, and community and organizational stakeholders. Consistent with the notion of empowerment and inclusiveness mentioned throughout this book, participants are drawn from a cross-section of relevant community and organizational networks.

The exact composition of the tables, with name tags for participants, may be arranged beforehand to obtain a diversity of perspective. The tables and work groups are labeled according to the different outcomes each will be working on throughout the event. For example a community that is seeking to enhance family stability may have one or more tables working on such outcomes as decreased caregiver stress, increased parenting skills, job readiness, and keeping families together.

POSTING GROUP INFORMATION

There should be ample space on two adjacent walls to post the participants' maps of current and future performance strategies and stations for posting the common data and outcome data mentioned earlier. There should also be ample table or floor space for participants to work on constructing the mental maps that capture both present and future performance strategies. Flip charts will also be necessary for the various groups to work on various agenda items during the event.

MATERIALS

The materials needed for any successful planning or community action event—markers, flip charts, and masking tape for hanging group results—should be provided either by the host organization or the facilitators. In addition, there should be posters or flip-chart pages hung in the room containing the general welcome, the day's agenda, and the ground rules. Near the entrance, there can be a table with the necessary registration materials.

Any preset exercise materials used for the event should be placed in sufficient supply at the various tables or included in the participants' registration packets. Registration packets should also include an agenda, a copy of the ground rules, evaluation forms, and other pertinent materials for the various sessions.

AMENITIES

The group organizing the event should consider what refreshments, if any, to provide or furnish participants with information about what is available (a nearby snack bar or cafeteria or vending machines). In light of this health-conscious age, those electing to provide some refreshments should try to offer enough choices to accommodate most participants (for example, both caffeinated and noncaffeinated beverages, fat-free, sugar-free snack foods; meals with meatless alternatives). Participants will need information about the location of nearby rest rooms and where and when smoking is permitted.

LUNCH

For large groups, it is preferable to have lunch provided on site. This helps to ensure that the group can be reassembled in a timely fashion. A well-organized community group will generally experience little difficulty in getting a local business, hospital, or service organization to provide the meal. The more the group is able to make and pay for its own arrangements, the greater the sense of ownership it will have of the process and subsequent decisions.

Postdialogue Debriefings

After the self-governance dialogue, the facilitators and the host organization conduct a debriefing. The purpose of this debriefing is to gather general feedback on the event itself, including participants' feedback on the facilitation, as well as to emphasize several points about the process of ongoing self-governance. This feedback is provided either to a community or organizational management team or to an emerging or existing performance team that will have ongoing responsibility for the process. Elements of the debriefing include

- Tying together loose ends
- Finalizing plans about community accountability
- Assigning community and organizational homework
- Developing outcomes-based training and technical assistance
- Planning for review of progress

GENERAL FEEDBACK

General feedback includes processing general impressions of how the dialogue went, including what worked and what did not seem to work. The facilitators provide feedback to the performance team on points of unresolved business, observations about the depth and meaningfulness of the dialogue, and gaps in the dialogue that need to be addressed for the process to work. Participants also provide feedback to facilitators about their effectiveness.

COMMUNITY ACCOUNTABILITY

Facilitators and the host organization review plans for ensuring public accountability for outcomes. Issues of who will do what, when, where, and how are discussed. The commitment to public accountability keeps the vision in front of the community through periodic reports of progress on critical outcomes. Facilitators and the host organization may also review and discuss tips and experiences from other communities.

COMMUNITY AND ORGANIZATIONAL HOMEWORK

The self-governance dialogue brings together a cross-section of community representatives. The work groups formed during the dialogue can and often do provide both a beginning sketch of an action plan and the nucleus of an ongoing performance team to monitor the process and outcomes. The facilitators and the host organization review plans to build on what was begun during the event through ongoing community and organizational homework.

TRAINING AND TECHNICAL ASSISTANCE

The process of mapping present and future outcomes can also provide a blueprint for linking them to training and technical assistance. The facilitators and host organization review these blueprints to identify where the process needs to be improved with the support of training and technical assistance. This training and technical assistance may focus on such things as:

- The role of information technology and automation for change

- Changing the organizational culture and value sets

- Building team work

REVIEW OF PROGRESS

Improving outcomes for families and children through self-governance is an ongoing learning process. It is most effective when it is not left to chance. The facilitators and the host organization review plans for conducting periodic change and performance reunions. These reunions provide opportunities to review progress made in reaching community outcomes and the performance strategies employed to secure those outcomes. The process is an open and public one, holding up for everyone's critical review and learning the successes, failures, and plans for the future. The reunions also provide opportunities to celebrate successes and rekindle the spirit and motivation that are integral to continued success.

Self-Governance Time Line

A time line for scheduling self-governance dialogues is presented in Figure 9. The time line identifies tasks, participants, and recommended target dates.

FIGURE 9: **Self-Governance Dialogue Timeline**

TASK	PARTICIPANTS	TARGET DATES
Preparation for Initial Planning Meeting • Secure facilitator • Identify and invite planning team members • Schedule a time and a place for initial planning meeting	Instigators	3 months before self-governance event
Initial Planning Meeting • Conduct preliminary assessment • Develop inclusive list of participants • Form a performance team • Finalize agenda • Assign tasks (see "Setting up the Event Dialogue: Logistics & Site")	Host organization/ planning team and facilitator	2 months before self-governance event
Self-Governance Event • Building community • Self-Governance • Common reality • Looking back • Paradigm shifts • Create the future • Community promises • Accountability	Facilitator, planning team, community members	2- to 2½-day self-governance event
Post-Event Debriefing • Tie up loose ends • Plan for community accountability • Assign homework • Schedule training and technical assistance • Plan progress reviews	Planning team/ performance team, facilitator	1 week after the self-governance event
Ongoing Change • Follow through on community accountability plan • Homework • Training and technical assistance • Progress reviews	Performance team, performance partnerships, and community	Ongoing

About The Jordan Institute for Families

The Jordan Institute for Families is a new resource for North Carolina and the nation. Named for one of North Carolina's most prominent families in recognition of support from Michael Jordan, the Jordan Institute at the School of Social Work at the University of North Carolina has one goal: to strengthen families. The Institute cuts across traditional disciplinary lines to bring together the best educational, public service, and research activities that focus on helping families become healthy and stable. The Institute provides technical assistance, training, and vital knowledge to program leaders and policymakers and promotes the development of innovative programs and services.

The Institute brings together scholars and leaders from organizations and campuses across the state and nation to

- Develop creative solutions to challenges facing families and communities

- Explore and share throughout the state and nation those practices and policies that strengthen families

- Promote public policies and programs that build resilient families

- Encourage informed debate about diverse approaches for strengthening families and their communities

For additional information on the Jordan Institute for Families call or write:

Gary M. Nelson, Associate Director
Jordan Institute for Families
School of Social Work
University of North Carolina at Chapel Hill
Chapel Hill, NC 27599-3550
Tele: (919) 962-4370
Fax: (919) 962-3653
E-mail: gmnelson@email.unc.edu

REFERENCES

INTRODUCTION

Argyris, C. (1992). *On Organizational Learning.* Cambridge, MA: Blackwell.

Schorr, L.B. (1997). *Common Purpose: Strengthening Families and Neighborhoods to Rebuild America.* New York: Doubleday.

CHAPTER 1

Bruner, C., Both, D., & Marzke, C. (1996). *Steps Along an Uncertain Path: State Initiatives Promoting Comprehensive, Community-Based Reform.* Des Moines, IA: National Center for Service Integration.

Ellinor, L., & Gerard, G. (1998). *Dialogue: Rediscover the Transforming Power of Conversation.* New York: John Wiley & Sons.

Osborne, D., & Plastrik, P. (1997). *Banishing Bureaucracy: The Five Strategies for Reinventing Government.* New York: Addison-Wesley.

Palmer, P.J. (1990). *The Active Life: Wisdom for Work, Creativity and Caring.* San Francisco: Harper & Row.

Schorr, L.B. (1997). *Common Purpose: Strengthening Families and Neighborhoods to Rebuild America.* New York: Doubleday.

Zohar, D. (1997). *Rewiring the Corporate Brain: Using the New Science to Rethink How We Structure and Lead Organizations.* San Francisco: Berrett-Koehler.

CHAPTER 2

Block, P. (1993). *Stewardship: Choosing Service Over Self-Interest.* San Francisco: Berrett-Koehler.

Linden, R.M. (1994). *Seamless Government: A Practical Guide to Re-Engineering in the Public Sector.* San Francisco: Jossey-Bass.

Pinchot, G., & Pinchot, E. (1993). *The End of Bureaucracy and the Rise of the Intelligent Organization.* San Francisco: Berrett-Koehler.

Schorr, L.B. (1997). *Common Purpose: Strengthening Families and Neighborhoods to Rebuild America.* New York: Doubleday.

de Tocqueville, A. (1990). *Democracy in America: Volumes 1 and 2.* New York: Vintage Books.

Wheatley, M.J. (1992). *Leadership and the New Science: Learning about Organization from an Orderly Universe.* San Francisco: Berrett-Koehler.

CHAPTER 3

Argyris, C. (1992). *On Organizational Learning.* Cambridge, MA: Blackwell.

Bohm, D. (1995). *Wholeness and the Implicate Order.* London: Routledge.

Ellinor, L., & Gerard, G. (1998). *Dialogue: Rediscover the Transforming Power of Conversation.* New York: John Wiley & Sons.

Hardin, G. (1968). "The Tragedy of the Commons." *Science, 162,*1243–1248.

Magaziner, E. (1995). The Way to Community. In Kazimierz Gozdz, (Ed.), *Community Building in Business: Renewing Spirit and Learning* (pp. 165–173). San Francisco: New Leaders Press.

Ostrom, E. (1990). *Governing the Commons: The Evolution of Institutions for Collective Action.* Cambridge, England: Cambridge University Press.

CHAPTER 4

Emery, M., & Purser, R.E. (1996). *The Search Conference: A Powerful Method for Planning Organizational Change and Community Action.* San Francisco: Jossey-Bass.

Jacobs, R.W. (1994). *Real Time Strategic Change: How to Involve the Entire Organization in Fast and Far Reaching Change.* San Francisco: Berrett-Koehler.

Weisbord, M.R., & Janoff, S. (1995). *Future Search: An Action Guide to Finding Common Ground in Organizations and Communities.* San Francisco: Berrett-Koehler.

CHAPTER 5

O'Murchu, D. (1997). *Quantum Theology.* New York: Crossroads.

Winnicott, D.W (1971). *Playing and Reality.* London: Tavistock Publications.

CHAPTER 6

de Geus, A. (1997). *The Living Company: Habits for Survival in a Turbulent Business World.* Boston, MA: Harvard Business School Press.

Herbert, B. (1997, October 2). The Keys to Cutting Crime. *The New York Times.* >

Kuhn, T.W. (1970). *The Structure of the Scientific Revolution* (2nd ed.). Chicago: The University of Chicago Press.

Piaget, J. (1986). *The Psychology of Intelligence.* London: Routledge & Kegan Paul.

Senge, P. (1990). *The Fifth Discipline.* New York. Doubleday/Currency.

CHAPTER 7

Kaplan, R.S., & Norton, D.P. (1996, January–February). Using the Balanced Scorecard as a Strategic Management System. *Harvard Business Review,* pp. 75–85.

Robinson, D.G., & Robinson, J.C. (1995). *Performance Consulting: Moving Beyond Training.* San Francisco: Berrett-Koehler.

CHAPTER 8

Harvard Business School. (1996). *NYPD New* (N9-396-293). Boston: Harvard Business School Publishing.

Senge, P., et al. (1999). <AQ2> *The Dance of Change: Challenges to Sustaining the Momentum in Learning Organizations.* New York: Doubleday.

Usher, C. L. (1995). Improving Evaluability Through Self-Evaluation. *Evaluation Practice,* 16(1), 59–68.

CHAPTER 9

DePree, M. (1989). *Leadership is an Art.* New York: Dell Publishing.

Frick, D.M., & Spears, L.C. (Eds.) (1996). *The Private Writings of Robert K. Greenleaf: On Becoming a Servant Leader.* San Francisco: Jossey-Bass.

Kofman, F., & Senge, P. (1993). Communities of Commitment: The Heart of Learning Organizations. *Organizational Dynamics.*

McKnight, J. (1995). *The Careless Society and Its Counterfeits.* New York: Basic Books.

Nair, K. (1997). *A Higher Standard of Leadership: Lessons from the Life of Gandhi.* San Francisco: Berrett-Koehler.

de Tocqueville, A. (1990). *Democracy in America: Volumes 1 and 2.* New York: Vintage Books.

Senge, P. et. al. (1999). *The Dance of Change.* New York. Doubleday/Currency.

CHAPTER 10

Covey, S.R. (1997). *The Seven Habits of Highly Effective Families.* New York: Golden Books.

Etzioni, A. (1996). *The New Golden Rule: Community and Morality in a Democratic Society.* New York: Basic Books.

Maslow, A. (1999).

de Tocqueville, A. (1990). *Democracy in America: Volumes 1 and 2.* New York: Vintage Books.

Senge, P. et. al. (1999). *The Dance of Change.* New York. Doubleday/Currency.

INDEX

About the Author

Gary M. Nelson, DSW, is an Associate Director for Program Development and Training with the Jordan Institute for Families at the University of North Carolina School of Social Work at Chapel Hill. Within the institute, he is the Director of the Family and Children's Resource Program and of the Center for Aging Research and Educational Services. He is also currently the Director of the National Alliance for Families, a partnership and reform initiative that benefits communities and families in North Carolina. Members of the alliance include the Family Resource Coalition of America, the Child Welfare League of America, the Jordan Institute for Families, and the North Carolina Division of Social Services.

Self-Governance in Communities and Families embodies his philosophy of program management and community development. The philosophy is reflected in his broad system reform work through the Jordan Institute for Families and his work as a consultant.

In recent years he, along with a small group of colleagues, has facilitated self-governance dialogues around outcomes for communities and families. Together they have formed the Self-Governance Group, a consulting and facilitation team. They offer a range of dialogue, facilitation and training services focused on empowering communities and their families. For information on the Self-Governance Group e-mail or write:

Self-Governance Group
P.O. Box 1368
Chapel Hill, North Carolina 27514–1368
E-Mail: selfgovernance@mindspring.com
Internet: http://www.selfgovernance.com
Phone: (919) 260-1290